SIMPLY THE BEST
RICE COOKER RECIPES
MARIAN GETZ

INTRODUCTION BY WOLFGANG PUCK

ACKNOWLEDGMENTS

A most sincere thank you to our wonderful viewers and customers for without you there would be no need for a cookbook. I try very hard to give you an array of recipes suited for the particular kitchen tool the cookbook is written for. Wolfgang and I create recipes faster than we can write them down. That is what chefs do and is also the reason to tune in to the live shows and even record them so you can learn new dishes that may not be in our cookbooks yet.

Thank you most of all to Wolfgang. You are the most passionate chef I know and it has been a privilege to work for you since 1998. You are a great leader and friend. Your restaurants are full of cooks and staff that have been with you for 20 or more years which is a true testament to how you lead us. Thanks for allowing me to write these cookbooks and for letting me share the stage at HSN with you.

To Greg, my sweet husband since 1983. Working together is a dream and I love you. You have taught me what a treasure it is to have a home filled with laughter.

To my boys, Jordan and Ben, we have a beautiful life, don't we? And it just keeps on getting better since we added Lindsay, J.J. as well as precious Easton and Sadie, our first grand babies.

To all the great people at WP Productions, Syd, Arnie, Mike, Phoebe, Michael, Nicolle, Tracy, Genevieve, Gina, Nancy, Sylvain and the rest of the team, you are all amazing to work with. Watching all the wonderful items we sell develop from idea to final product on live television is an awe-inspiring process to see and I love that I get to be a part of it.

To Daniel Koren, our patient editor and photographer, thank you for your dedication. You make the photo shoot days fun and you are such an easygoing person to work with in the cramped, hot studio we have to share. We have learned so much together and have far more to learn.

To Greg, Cat, Estela, Angi, Laurie, Keith, Maribel and Margarita who are the most dedicated, loving staff anyone could wish for. You are the true heroes behind the scenes. You are a well-oiled machine of very hard working people who pull off the live shows at HSN. It is a magical production to watch, from the first box unpacked, to the thousands of eggs cracked and beaten to running to get that "thing" Wolf asks for at the last minute, to the very last dish washed and put away it is quite a sight to behold. I love you all and I deeply love what we do.

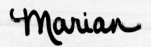

The modern tools we have in the kitchen, whether in the restaurant or at home, are expected to be able to do more than one thing. While a rice cooker is typically thought of as an appliance that can only cook rice, my rice cooker is capable of cooking a wide variety of foods including breakfast, lunch, dinner, dessert and much more.

The rice cooker is the perfect multi-tasker. The simple 1-touch operation and nonstick insert allow for cooking a variety of foods with ease.

Marian's "Simply The Best Rice Cooker Recipes" cookbook is the perfect match for my rice cooker. She has done an amazing job at writing recipes that will even make a novice cook feel like a pro. Over the years, Marian has proven to me to be a very reliable resource. I admire her experience in the kitchen, both in the restaurant and at home. While she likes making challenging dishes, she is also comfortable preparing everyday meals that her family loves to eat. The rice cooker is the perfect kitchen helper for making both, which lead her to write this cookbook.

As I learned long ago, alongside my mother and grandmother, you should always put lots of love into everything you cook. This is certainly evident in this cookbook.

INTRODUCTION BY WOLFGANG PUCK

RECIPES

TABLE OF CONTENTS

4

TABLE OF CONTENTS

RICE COOKER TIPS

Your Wolfgang Puck rice cooker may be small but it can do great things for you. It's quiet, fast, efficient and one of the easiest kitchen appliances to use. About 40% of homes in the USA have a household of two or less so this appliance is on point for how many of us currently live.

MEASURING CUP

An American standard 1 cup measure holds 8 ounces. A Japanese or Chinese standard cup holds 6 ounces and measures 3/4 cup. The measuring cup that comes with your rice cooker holds 6 ounces (3/4 cup) and is not used for any of the recipes in this cookbook. For these recipes use the standard American style measuring cups and spoons that you already have. Also, you will notice abbreviations in the ingredient charts for this book. TBSP stands for tablespoon and tsp stands for teaspoon.

HANDLING INGREDIENTS

As a general rule, ensure that ingredients do not exceed the MAX line marking on the inside of your rice cooker insert. Some exceptions would be foods that wilt down when cooked such as fresh spinach. If your ingredients are low inside the rice cooker and you jostle the appliance accidentally, you can inadvertently switch the unit from COOK to WARM mode. Look at the rice cooker once in a while and make sure the COOK light is on and not the WARM light. Also if you want to melt a tablespoon of butter or a small amount of another ingredient, you will need to close the lid to keep the rice cooker in COOK mode. When cooking foods that contain a larger amount of milk or cream, set the rice cooker on a stable sheet pan before beginning to cook as these ingredients have a tendency to boil over. This is true for any of the ways we cook with them and holds true for the rice cooker as well. If you experience a boil over, the sheet pan will make clean up easier. If a boil over occurs, please refer to the manual how to disassemble and clean your rice cooker. For foods like oatmeal, cream of wheat, grits and pasta sauce with meatballs, cover your hands with potholders or a kitchen towel while stirring or serving. These foods are thick enough that the hot bubbles can potentially reach the top of the rice cooker insert and cause burns.

COOKING

Cooking easy, delicious and healthful meals is so easy with this little gadget. In almost all of the recipes in this book, you simply add the ingredients to the rice cooker, give them a stir, close the lid, press the COOK button and set a kitchen timer or smart phone timer to keep track of time. The average cooking time for the recipes in this book is 20-25 minutes and this is unattended time so you are free to accomplish other household tasks while your meal cooks itself. Many foods can also be cooked on WARM mode which operates at slightly over 180°F. It is a safe way to gently cook foods without risking bacteria to grow or foods to spoil. It is a low and slow way to cook similar to a slow cooker. In recipes that use very oily or sweet ingredients (excluding baked items), the rice cooker might switch to WARM early. If this happens, either stir the ingredients or add some additional liquid and stir then press COOK again to continue cooking.

ADDITIONAL COOKING TIME

One of my favorite things about the rice cooker is that it is a very "forgiving" way to cook. If your rice or pasta is not quite done to your liking, simply add a bit more liquid, press COOK again and cook for a few more minutes until you like it. I think that is the reason this little appliance is so trusted in our kitchens.

RICE COOKING CHART

Please follow the below chart for cooking the most common types of rice:

| | 1.5 CUP | | 3 CUP | | 5 CUP | | |
	RICE	WATER	RICE	WATER	RICE	WATER	COOK TIME
BROWN RICE	1 CUP	1 CUP + 2 TBSP	2 CUPS	2 1/4 CUPS	3 CUPS	3 1/4 CUPS + 2 TBSP	45 MIN
WILD RICE	1/2 CUP	1 1/4 CUPS	1 CUP	2 1/2 CUPS	1 1/2 CUPS	3 3/4 CUPS	55 MIN
BLACK RICE*	1 CUP	1 1/2 CUPS	2 CUPS	3 CUPS	3 CUPS	4 1/2 CUPS	35 MIN
RED RICE	1 CUP	1 1/2 CUPS	2 CUPS	3 CUPS	3 CUPS	4 1/2 CUPS	35 MIN
SUSHI RICE	1 CUP	1 CUP	2 CUPS	2 CUPS	3 CUPS	3 CUPS	25 MIN
BASMATI RICE	1 CUP	1 CUP	2 CUPS	2 CUPS	3 CUPS	3 CUPS	25 MIN
LONG GRAIN	1 CUP	1 CUP + 2 TBSP	2 CUPS	2 1/4 CUPS	3 CUPS	3 1/4 CUPS + 2 TBSP	25 MIN
INSTANT	1 CUP	1 CUP	2 CUPS	2 CUPS	3 CUPS	3 CUPS	25 MIN
CONVERTED	1 CUP	2 CUPS	2 CUPS	4 CUPS	3 CUPS	6 CUPS	25 MIN
YELLOW RICE*	1 PKG (5 OZ)	1 1/4 CUPS	2 PKGS (5 OZ EA)	2 1/2 CUPS	3 PKGS (5 OZ EA)	3 3/4 CUPS	25 MIN

*1 TBSP OIL   *2 TBSP OIL   *3 TBSP OIL

RICE COOKER MODEL

There are many rice cooker models on the market that come in different sizes. The recipes in this book provide instructions for three of the most popular rice cookers, the 1.5 cup, 3 cup and 5 cup models. Before starting a recipe, determine which size rice cooker model you own and follow the ingredient suggestion that correlate to your model then proceed to follow the method which is the same for all models.

BAKING

When baking in the rice cooker, you will notice that after about 6-7 minutes into the cooking cycle, the appliance switches to WARM mode, even though the contents are not cooked through yet. This occurs because the rice cooker has a sensor built in that operates at 212°F (the temperature at which water or other liquids boil). As soon as liquids get absorbed into the foods you are cooking (or when foods approach doneness), the temperature starts to climb. Once it passes 212°F the unit automatically switches to WARM and you are not able to switch it right back to COOK mode. When a crust starts to form during baking, the rice cooker assumes that all of the moisture in the recipe has dissipated and switches to WARM. In order to finish baking, simply wait 5-6 minutes while on WARM mode which allows the moisture in the food to seep to the bottom of the rice cooker insert again. Once this happens you will be able to push COOK and continue cooking. You might need to repeat this cycle until the contents are cooked through or desired doneness is achieved. In general, to test for doneness insert a wooden pick slightly off-center. When pulling it back out, it should emerge clean or with just a few moist crumbs clinging to it. A streak of shiny batter indicates more time is needed. To test doneness on a custard-based dessert, insert a small paring knife off-center, it should emerge clean. For yeast breads use a thermometer and cook to 195°F or a few degrees higher which indicates that the food is done. You will notice that the top of baked foods is a pale color. Don't worry, as soon as you invert the done food onto a serving plate, you will see the familiar golden brown color we associate with baked goods.

HIGH ALTITUDE COOKING

If you live in an area of high altitude, you might need to increase cooking times by up to 20% and adjust liquid ingredients as needed.

PREP ONCE - USE TWICE

Think about any meals you may want to cook during the upcoming week and prep for more than you need today. For example, if you're buying meat or chicken for today's meal, portion what is needed for the recipe today then package and label the remaining meat and put it in the freezer. That way it's easy to make the next meal with the leftover portion of meat.

CHICKEN

You will notice that this cookbook often makes use of chicken tenders or chicken tenderloins. I selected these because they are the leanest part of the chicken and require no trimming. They also fit easily inside this small rice cooker. They are raw and can be purchased fresh or frozen. You can use them from the frozen state in these recipes and expect the recipe to take an extra 5 minutes of cooking time. If the chicken tenders need to be diced, you can easily do this with a sturdy knife while they are still frozen.

BASES

Many recipes in this book call for the use of bases. My favorite one is called Better Than Bouillon and is sold in jars. It is available in many flavors including chicken, beef and vegetable. They are in a paste form, can easily be spooned from the jar and add a tremendous flavor to your food. Bases are a modern version of old-fashioned bouillon cubes. They are far better in flavor and much easier to transport, use and store than the large quart-size tetra packs of liquid stocks which are often watery. Also, unused boxes of stock must be refrigerated and often get tossed out which is a waste of money.

TIPS

SALT

The salt used in this book is Diamond Crystal Kosher Salt. It is half as salty as most other brands. This is because the grains are very fluffy and therefore not as many fit into a measuring spoon. This brand also lists only "salt" as the ingredient on the box. If you are using salt other than Diamond Crystal Kosher Salt, simply use half the amount specified in the recipe.

PANTRY

Being prepared to cook the recipes in this book, or any recipe for that matter, is one of the keys to success in the kitchen. Your pantry must be stocked with the basics. The list below includes some of the ingredients you will find in this book and some that we feel are important to always have on hand. It is not necessary to have all the items but it's advantageous to have a good selection in the kitchen.

PERISHABLES

Onions
Garlic
Tomatoes
Carrots
Celery
Ginger
Bell Peppers
White Potatoes
Sweet Potatoes
Squashes
Citrus
Apples
Bananas
Lettuce
Spinach
Fresh Herbs
Green Onions
Milk or Almond Milk
Cream Cheese
Parmesan Cheese
Yogurt

SPICES

Kosher Salt
Pepper
Bay Leaves
Sage
Oregano
Thyme
Chili Flakes
Cumin Seeds
Curry Powder
Onion Powder
Garlic Powder
Dry Mustard
Ground Cinnamon
Nutmeg
Cloves
Chili Powder

DRY GOODS

Sugars
Sugar Substitute
Vanilla
Extracts/Flavorings
Agave Syrup
Canned Tomatoes
Canned Beans
Canned Vegetables
Dried Chilies
Pasta
Lentils & Dried Beans
Bases or Stocks
Olives
Ketchup
Mustard
Pickles
Oils
Vinegar
Honey

MAC & CHEESE

	1.5 CUP (3 CUPS COOKED) 1-2 SERVINGS	3 CUP (6 CUPS COOKED) 3-4 SERVINGS	5 CUP (10 CUPS COOKED) 5-6 SERVINGS
ELBOW MACARONI, UNCOOKED	3/4 CUP	1 1/2 CUPS	2 1/4 CUPS
CHICKEN-FLAVORED BASE, STORE-BOUGHT	1 tsp	2 tsp	1 TBSP
WATER	3/4 CUP	1 1/2 CUPS	2 1/4 CUPS
HEAVY CREAM	1/2 CUP	1 CUP	1 1/2 CUPS
CHEDDAR CHEESE, SHREDDED	1/4 CUP	1/2 CUP	3/4 CUP
MOZZARELLA CHEESE, SHREDDED	1/4 CUP	1/2 CUP	3/4 CUP
PARMESAN CHEESE, SHREDDED	1 TBSP	2 TBSP	3 TBSP

Method:

1. *Combine all ingredients, except all cheeses, in the rice cooker and stir.*
2. *Close lid and press COOK.*
3. *When rice cooker switches to WARM (about 20-25 minutes), stir in the cheeses thoroughly.*
4. *Close lid and press COOK again (this is where the brown crust forms on the bottom).*
5. *When rice cooker switches to WARM again, remove, garnish as desired and serve.*

PERFECT
WHITE RICE

	1.5 CUP (3 CUPS COOKED) 1-2 SERVINGS	3 CUP (6 CUPS COOKED) 3-4 SERVINGS	5 CUP (10 CUPS COOKED) 5-6 SERVINGS
BASMATI WHITE RICE, UNCOOKED	1 1/2 CUPS	3 CUPS	5 CUPS
WATER	1 1/2 CUPS	3 CUPS	5 CUPS
KOSHER SALT (OPTIONAL)	TO TASTE	TO TASTE	TO TASTE

Method:

1. *Place rice in a strainer and wash under cold running water for 2-3 minutes while rubbing rice grains between your fingers. This will remove the sticky surface starch.*
2. *Drain rice then transfer to the rice cooker.*
3. *Add the water and salt to the rice cooker.*
4. *Close lid and press COOK.*
5. *Cooking is complete with rice cooker switches to WARM (about 20-25 minutes).*
6. *Let rice rest in the rice cooker on WARM for 10 minutes.*
7. *Remove and serve as desired.*

TIP

This recipe uses long-grain basmati white rice which has separate grains that are light and fluffy when cooked. Sushi rice is the opposite with short and sticky grains most commonly used in sushi (see recipe on page 90).

POT ROAST
FOR ONE

	1.5 CUP (3 CUPS COOKED) 1-2 SERVINGS	3 CUP (6 CUPS COOKED) 3-4 SERVINGS	5 CUP (10 CUPS COOKED) 5-6 SERVINGS
BEEF CHUCK, RAW, CUBED	8 OZ	1 POUND	1 1/2 POUNDS
SMALL YELLOW ONION, CHUNKED	1	2	3
SMALL CARROT, CHUNKED	1	2	3
SMALL CELERY STALK, CHUNKED	1	2	3
RED BLISS POTATO, CHUNKED	1	2	3
BEEF STOCK	1 CUP	2 CUPS	3 CUPS
BAY LEAF	1	2	3
SOY SAUCE	2 tsp	1 TBSP+1 tsp	2 TBSP
ALL PURPOSE FLOUR	2 tsp	1 TBSP+1 tsp	2 TBSP
KOSHER SALT AND FRESHLY GROUND PEPPER	TO TASTE	TO TASTE	TO TASTE

Method:

1. Combine all ingredients in the rice cooker but do not fill past the MAX line of your rice cooker insert (you may have some extra vegetables, use another time as desired).
2. Close lid and press COOK.
3. Cook for 1 1/2 hours or until beef is fork tender and gravy is thick and bubbly.
4. When cooking is complete, garnish as desired and serve.

PINEAPPLE
UPSIDE DOWN CAKE

	1.5 CUP (3 CUPS COOKED) 1-2 SERVINGS	3 CUP (6 CUPS COOKED) 3-4 SERVINGS	5 CUP (10 CUPS COOKED) 5-6 SERVINGS
MAPLE SYRUP	2 TBSP	1/4 CUP	1/3 CUP
PINEAPPLE RINGS	1	3	6
MARASCHINO CHERRIES	1	3	5
UNSALTED BUTTER	3 TBSP	6 TBSP	9 TBSP
LARGE EGGS	1	2	3
SOUR CREAM	1 TBSP	2 TBSP	3 TBSP
WHOLE MILK	3 TBSP	6 TBSP	9 TBSP
ALL PURPOSE FLOUR	1/4 CUP	1/2 CUP	3/4 CUP
BAKING POWDER	1/4 tsp	1/2 tsp	3/4 tsp
KOSHER SALT	1/4 tsp	1/2 tsp	3/4 tsp
VANILLA EXTRACT	1/4 tsp	1/2 tsp	3/4 tsp
GRANULATED SUGAR	1/4 CUP	1/2 CUP	3/4 CUP

Method:

1. Apply nonstick cooking spray to the rice cooker.
2. Pour syrup into the rice cooker then top with pineapple ring and add the cherry to the ring center.
3. In a mixing bowl, whisk together remaining ingredients until smooth.
4. Pour mixture over the rice cooker contents then close lid and press COOK.
5. When rice cooker switches to WARM (about 6-7 minutes), wait for 5-6 minutes then press COOK again; repeat if necessary.
6. Cooking is complete after 20-25 minutes or when a wooden pick inserted slightly off-center comes out with just a few moist crumbs clinging to it. The top of the cake should be pale and dull looking.
7. Invert onto a serving plate so that the brown part with pineapple is on top.
8. Garnish as desired and serve.

BONELESS BUFFALO
CHICKEN

	1.5 CUP (3 CUPS COOKED) 1-2 SERVINGS	3 CUP (6 CUPS COOKED) 3-4 SERVINGS	5 CUP (10 CUPS COOKED) 5-6 SERVINGS
CHICKEN TENDERS, RAW	6	12	18
BUFFALO WING SAUCE, BOTTLED	1/2 CUP	1 CUP	1 1/2 CUPS
CHICKEN STOCK	1/4 CUP	1/2 CUP	3/4 CUP
KOSHER SALT AND FRESHLY GROUND PEPPER	TO TASTE	TO TASTE	TO TASTE
BLUE CHEESE CRUMBLES	1/4 CUP	1/2 CUP	3/4 CUP
CELERY, THINLY SLICED	1 STALK	2 STALKS	3 STALKS

Method:

1. *Combine the chicken tenders, wing sauce, stock, salt and pepper in the rice cooker and stir.*
2. *Close lid and press COOK.*
3. *Cook for 20-25 minutes or until chicken is cooked through and sauce is bubbly.*
4. *Stir in the blue cheese until it melts and gets creamy.*
5. *Garnish as desired and serve hot with celery.*

BBQ BABY BACK
RIBS

	1.5 CUP (3 CUPS COOKED) 1-2 SERVINGS	3 CUP (6 CUPS COOKED) 3-4 SERVINGS	5 CUP (10 CUPS COOKED) 5-6 SERVINGS
BABY BACK RIBS, SLICED FROM RACK	4	8	12
KOSHER SALT AND FRESHLY GROUND PEPPER	TO TASTE	TO TASTE	TO TASTE
CHICKEN STOCK OR BEER	1/2 CUP	1 CUP	1 1/2 CUPS
BBQ SAUCE, BOTTLED	1/2 CUP	1 CUP	1 1/2 CUPS

Method:

1. *Combine all ingredients in the rice cooker.*
2. *Close lid and press COOK.*
3. *Cook for 45 minutes or until ribs are tender and sauce is thick and bubbly.*
4. *When cooking is complete, garnish as desired and serve.*

TIP
If the BBQ sauce you're using is very sweet, the rice cooker might switch to WARM early. If this happens just add a bit more liquid such as stock or beer and continue cooking.

15

VEGGIE OMELET

	1.5 CUP (3 CUPS COOKED) 1-2 SERVINGS	3 CUP (6 CUPS COOKED) 3-4 SERVINGS	5 CUP (10 CUPS COOKED) 5-6 SERVINGS
UNSALTED BUTTER, MELTED	1 TBSP	2 TBSP	3 TBSP
LARGE EGGS, BEATEN	2	4	6
KOSHER SALT AND FRESHLY GROUND PEPPER	TO TASTE	TO TASTE	TO TASTE
GREEN ONION, SLICED	1	2	3
GRAPE TOMATOES, HALVED	4	8	12
CHEDDAR CHEESE, SHREDDED	2 TBSP	1/4 CUP	1/3 CUP

Method:

1. *Pour the butter in the rice cooker.*
2. *In a bowl, whisk together remaining ingredients then pour into the rice cooker.*
3. *Close lid and press COOK.*
4. *Cook for 5-7 minutes or until eggs are just set.*
5. *When cooking is complete, invert onto a plate, garnish as desired and serve.*

TIP

This omelet is a great place to use up any leftover cooked vegetables you might have in your fridge.

BEEF
STROGANOFF

	1.5 CUP (3 CUPS COOKED) 1-2 SERVINGS	3 CUP (6 CUPS COOKED) 3-4 SERVINGS	5 CUP (10 CUPS COOKED) 5-6 SERVINGS
BEEF STEW PIECES, RAW, THINLY SLICED	4 OZ	8 OZ	12 OZ
EGG NOODLES, UNCOOKED	1/2 CUP	1 CUP	1 1/2 CUPS
BEEF STOCK	1/2 CUP	1 CUP	1 1/2 CUPS
KOSHER SALT AND FRESHLY GROUND PEPPER	TO TASTE	TO TASTE	TO TASTE
YELLOW ONION, THINLY SLICED	1/4 CUP	1/2 CUP	3/4 CUP
DILL PICKLE RELISH	1 TBSP	2 TBSP	3 TBSP
SOUR CREAM AND CHOPPED DILL FOR SERVING	AS DESIRED	AS DESIRED	AS DESIRED

Method:

1. *Combine all ingredients, except sour cream and dill, in the rice cooker and stir.*
2. *Close lid and press COOK.*
3. *Cook for 30 minutes or until beef and noodles are tender.*
4. *When cooking is complete, garnish as desired and serve hot with sour cream and dill.*

SALTED CARAMEL
MONKEY BREAD

	1.5 CUP (3 CUPS COOKED) 1-2 SERVINGS	3 CUP (6 CUPS COOKED) 3-4 SERVINGS	5 CUP (10 CUPS COOKED) 5-6 SERVINGS
UNSALTED BUTTER, MELTED	2 TBSP	1/4 CUP	1/3 CUP
GRANULATED SUGAR	2 TBSP	1/4 CUP	1/3 CUP
GROUND CINNAMON	1 tsp	2 tsp	1 TBSP
KOSHER SALT	A PINCH	2 PINCHES	3 PINCHES
FROZEN DINNER ROLL DOUGH BALLS, RAW (GOLF BALL SIZE)	6	12	18
PECAN PIECES FOR SERVING	AS DESIRED	AS DESIRED	AS DESIRED

Method:

1. *Apply nonstick cooking spray to the rice cooker and keep unit unplugged.*
2. *Pour half of the melted butter into the rice cooker.*
3. *Sprinkle half the sugar and cinnamon as well as a pinch of salt over the butter in the rice cooker.*
4. *Place the dough balls into the rice cooker.*
5. *Drizzle dough balls with remaining butter, cinnamon, sugar and additional salt.*
6. *While unit is still unplugged, cover with lid, let rest for 40 minutes or until puffed then plug in and press COOK.*
7. *When rice cooker switches to WARM (about 6-7 minutes), let rest for 5-6 minutes then press COOK again.*
8. *When rice cooker switches to WARM again, set a kitchen timer for 15 minutes.*
9. *After 15 minutes press tops, they should spring back and be dull tan in color; cook for a few more minutes if needed.*
10. *Invert onto a small serving plate so that the brown part is on top.*
11. *Top with pecans, garnish as desired and serve.*

SMOTHERED
CHICKEN BREAST

	1.5 CUP (3 CUPS COOKED) 1-2 SERVINGS	3 CUP (6 CUPS COOKED) 3-4 SERVINGS	5 CUP (10 CUPS COOKED) 5-6 SERVINGS
CHICKEN STOCK	1/2 CUP	1 CUP	1 1/2 CUPS
ALL PURPOSE FLOUR	2 tsp	1 TBSP+1 tsp	2 TBSP
CHICKEN BREAST, SMALL, UNCOOKED	2	4	6
SMALL YELLOW ONION, SLICED	1	2	3
GROUND SAGE	1/4 tsp	1/2 tsp	3/4 tsp
UNSALTED BUTTER	1 TBSP	2 TBSP	3 TBSP
KOSHER SALT AND FRESHLY GROUND PEPPER	TO TASTE	TO TASTE	TO TASTE

Method:

1. *In a small mixing bowl, whisk together the stock and flour until smooth.*
2. *Pour stock mixture and remaining ingredients into the rice cooker.*
3. *Close lid and press COOK.*
4. *Cook for 25-30 minutes or until chicken is fork tender and gravy is thick and bubbly.*
5. *When cooking is complete, garnish as desired and serve.*

VEGAN PEANUT BUTTER
LAVA CAKE

	1.5 CUP (3 CUPS COOKED) 1-2 SERVINGS	3 CUP (6 CUPS COOKED) 3-4 SERVINGS	5 CUP (10 CUPS COOKED) 5-6 SERVINGS
COCONUT OIL OR CANOLA OIL	2 TBSP	1/4 CUP	1/3 CUP
GRANULATED SUGAR	1/3 CUP	2/3 CUP	1 CUP
ALMOND OR SOY MILK	1/2 CUP	1 CUP	1 1/2 CUPS
APPLE CIDER VINEGAR	1 1/2 tsp	1 TBSP	1 1/2 TBSP
ALL PURPOSE FLOUR	3/4 CUP	1 1/2 CUPS	2 1/4 CUPS
COCOA POWDER	2 TBSP	1/4 CUP	1/3 CUP
VANILLA EXTRACT	1/2 tsp	1 tsp	1 1/2 tsp
KOSHER SALT	1/4 tsp	1/2 tsp	3/4 tsp
BAKING SODA	1/2 tsp	1 tsp	1 1/2 tsp
PEANUT BUTTER, MICROWAVED UNTIL LIQUID	1 TBSP	2 TBSP	3 TBSP

Method:

1. *In a mixing bowl, stir together all ingredients, except peanut butter, until blended.*
2. *Apply nonstick cooking spray to the rice cooker then pour in the mixture.*
3. *Close lid and press COOK.*
4. *After 6-7 minutes of cooking, the rice cooker will switch to WARM.*
5. *The cake is not baked at this point, wait 5-6 minutes then press COOK again.*
6. *When the cake has a ring of obviously cooked cake around the perimeter (after about 15 minutes of cooking), spoon the liquid peanut butter into the center of the still shiny batter. Gently nudge it down until the chocolate batter covers the peanut butter.*
7. *Close lid and allow cake to cook for an additional 10 minutes or until the top of the cake just becomes dull with very little shiny batter at the cake center remaining. Do not overcook this cake or the peanut butter center will not remain liquid.*
8. *When cooking is complete, unmold onto serving platter then cut into the cake and let the "lava" flow out.*

BOURBON
CHICKEN TENDERS

	1.5 CUP (3 CUPS COOKED) 1-2 SERVINGS	3 CUP (6 CUPS COOKED) 3-4 SERVINGS	5 CUP (10 CUPS COOKED) 5-6 SERVINGS
CHICKEN TENDERS, RAW	3	6	9
LIGHT BROWN SUGAR	1/4 CUP	1/2 CUP	3/4 CUP
BOURBON	1 TBSP	2 TBSP	3 TBSP
CHICKEN STOCK	1/3 CUP	2/3 CUP	1 CUP
OYSTER SAUCE, BOTTLED	2 tsp	4 tsp	2 TBSP
SOY SAUCE	1 TBSP	2 TBSP	3 TBSP
GARLIC CLOVES, CHOPPED	2	4	6
FRESH GINGER COINS, CHOPPED	2	4	6
CORNSTARCH	1 TBSP	2 TBSP	3 TBSP
PERFECT WHITE RICE (SEE PAGE 11) FOR SERVING	AS DESIRED	AS DESIRED	AS DESIRED
GREEN ONION, JULIENNED	1	2	3

Method:

1. *Combine all ingredients, except rice and green onions, in the rice cooker and stir.*
2. *Close lid and press COOK.*
3. *Cook for 20 minutes or until chicken is cooked through and sauce is bubbly.*
4. *When cooking is complete, garnish as desired and serve with rice and green onions.*

TIP
This recipe is similar to the popular bourbon chicken available in most mall food courts across the country.

OATMEAL WITH
BERRIES

	1.5 CUP (3 CUPS COOKED) 1-2 SERVINGS	3 CUP (6 CUPS COOKED) 3-4 SERVINGS	5 CUP (10 CUPS COOKED) 5-6 SERVINGS
OLD FASHIONED ROLLED OATS	1 CUP	2 CUPS	3 CUPS
WATER	1 CUP	2 CUPS	3 CUPS
WHOLE MILK OR ALMOND MILK	1/2 CUP	1 CUP	1 1/2 CUPS
KOSHER SALT	A PINCH	2 PINCHES	3 PINCHES
MAPLE SYRUP	2 TBSP	1/4 CUP	1/3 CUP
MIXED BERRIES	1/4 CUP	1/2 CUP	3/4 CUP

Method:

1. Combine all ingredients, except berries, in the rice cooker.
2. Stir well, close lid and press COOK.
3. Cook for 20-25 minutes or until mixture is thick and bubbly, stirring occasionally using a potholder.
4. When cooking is complete, top with berries, garnish as desired and serve.

CHEESE GRITS

	1.5 CUP (3 CUPS COOKED) 1-2 SERVINGS	3 CUP (6 CUPS COOKED) 3-4 SERVINGS	5 CUP (10 CUPS COOKED) 5-6 SERVINGS
QUICK COOKING GRITS	1/3 CUP	2/3 CUP	1 CUP
WATER	1 CUP	2 CUPS	3 CUPS
KOSHER SALT AND FRESHLY GROUND PEPPER	TO TASTE	TO TASTE	TO TASTE
SHARP CHEDDAR CHEESE, SHREDDED	1/3 CUP	2/3 CUP	1 CUP

Method:

1. *Combine all ingredients, except cheese, in the rice cooker and stir.*
2. *Close lid and press COOK.*
3. *Cook for 20 minutes or until rice cooker switches to WARM, stirring occasionally using a potholder.*
4. *Carefully add the cheese and stir thoroughly until cheese is melted.*
5. *Garnish as desired and serve.*

TIP

If substituting old fashioned or coarse ground grits for quick cooking grits, cook for an additional 5-10 minutes.

CHICKEN & BROCCOLI
PASTA

	1.5 CUP (3 CUPS COOKED) 1-2 SERVINGS	3 CUP (6 CUPS COOKED) 3-4 SERVINGS	5 CUP (10 CUPS COOKED) 5-6 SERVINGS
SMALL PASTA, UNCOOKED	1/2 CUP	1 CUP	1 1/2 CUPS
CHICKEN TENDERS, RAW, DICED	3	6	9
GARLIC CLOVES, CHOPPED	3	6	9
JARRED PEPPERONCINI PEPPERS, CHOPPED	1 TBSP	2 TBSP	3 TBSP
BRINE FROM PEPPERONCINI JAR	1 TBSP	2 TBSP	3 TBSP
KOSHER SALT AND FRESHLY GROUND PEPPER	TO TASTE	TO TASTE	TO TASTE
CHICKEN STOCK	1/2 CUP	1 CUP	1 1/2 CUPS
CORNSTARCH	1 TBSP	2 TBSP	3 TBSP
RED BELL PEPPERS, JULIENNED	1/4 CUP	1/2 CUP	3/4 CUP
BROCCOLI FLORETS, FRESH OR FROZEN	1/3 CUP	2/3 CUP	1 CUP

Method:

1. Combine all ingredients in the rice cooker and stir.
2. Close lid and press COOK.
3. Cook for 20-25 minutes or until pasta is tender, stirring occasionally.
4. Spoon into bowls, garnish as desired and serve.

TIP

If you prefer crisp tender broccoli, add it after 15 minutes of cooking.

CONFETTI BIRTHDAY CAKE

	1.5 CUP (3 CUPS COOKED) 1-2 SERVINGS	3 CUP (6 CUPS COOKED) 3-4 SERVINGS	5 CUP (10 CUPS COOKED) 5-6 SERVINGS
UNSALTED BUTTER, MELTED	3 TBSP	1/4 CUP + 2 TBSP	1/2 CUP + 1 TBSP
LARGE EGG, BEATEN	1	2	3
SOUR CREAM	1 TBSP	2 TBSP	3 TBSP
WHOLE MILK	3 TBSP	1/4 CUP + 2 TBSP	1/2 CUP + 1 TBSP
ALL PURPOSE FLOUR	1/4 CUP	1/2 CUP	3/4 CUP
BAKING POWDER	1/4 tsp	1/2 tsp	3/4 tsp
KOSHER SALT	1/4 tsp	1/2 tsp	3/4 tsp
GRANULATED SUGAR	1/4 CUP	1/2 CUP	3/4 CUP
VANILLA EXTRACT	1/4 tsp	1/2 tsp	3/4 tsp
CONFETTI SPRINKLES	1 TBSP	2 TBSP	3 TBSP

Method:

1. *Apply nonstick cooking spray to the rice cooker.*
2. *Combine all ingredients in the rice cooker; whisk until smooth.*
3. *Close lid and press COOK.*
4. *When rice cooker switches to WARM (about 6-7 minutes), wait for 5-6 minutes then press COOK again; repeat if necessary.*
5. *Cooking is complete after about 20 minutes of cooking or when a wooden pick inserted slightly off-center comes out with just a few moist crumbs clinging to it.*
6. *When cooking is complete, remove from rice cooker and invert onto a small serving plate so that the brown part is on top.*
7. *Garnish as desired and serve.*

TIP

You can make a chocolate version of this cake by using chocolate jimmies or sprinkles instead of the confetti sprinkles.

EASIEST BUTTERED
NOODLES

	1.5 CUP (3 CUPS COOKED) 1-2 SERVINGS	3 CUP (6 CUPS COOKED) 3-4 SERVINGS	5 CUP (10 CUPS COOKED) 5-6 SERVINGS
PASTA OF YOUR CHOICE, UNCOOKED	1 1/2 CUPS	3 CUPS	4 1/2 CUPS
WATER	1 CUP	2 CUPS	3 CUPS
KOSHER SALT	TO TASTE	TO TASTE	TO TASTE
UNSALTED BUTTER	2 TBSP	1/4 CUP	1/3 CUP
CHOPPED PARSLEY FOR SERVING	AS DESIRED	AS DESIRED	AS DESIRED

Method:

1. *Combine all ingredients, except parsley, in the rice cooker and stir.*
2. *Close lid and press COOK.*
3. *Cooking is complete when rice cooker switches to WARM (about 20-25 minutes).*
4. *Top with parsley, garnish as desired and serve.*

TACO
BAKE

	1.5 CUP (3 CUPS COOKED) 1-2 SERVINGS	3 CUP (6 CUPS COOKED) 3-4 SERVINGS	5 CUP (10 CUPS COOKED) 5-6 SERVINGS
CHICKEN TENDERS, DICED, RAW	3	6	9
TACO SEASONING	TO TASTE	TO TASTE	TO TASTE
SOFT CORN TORTILLAS, TORN	4	8	12
CANNED TOMATOES WITH GREEN CHILIES (11 OZ SIZE)	1 CAN	2 CANS	3 CANS
MEXICAN BLEND CHEESE, SHREDDED	1/2 CUP	1 CUP	1 1/2 CUPS
FRESH CILANTRO AND TORTILLA CHIPS FOR SERVING	AS DESIRED	AS DESIRED	AS DESIRED

Method:

1. Combine all ingredients, except cilantro and chips, in the rice cooker and stir well.
2. Close lid and press COOK.
3. Cook for 20-25 minutes or until chicken is cooked through.
4. When cooking is complete, garnish as desired and serve with cilantro and chips.

TIP
You can make this recipe using ground beef or ground pork as well. The cooking times will be the same.

FLAN
FOR ONE

INGREDIENTS FOR THE CARAMEL

	1.5 CUP (3 CUPS COOKED) 1-2 SERVINGS	3 CUP (6 CUPS COOKED) 3-4 SERVINGS	5 CUP (10 CUPS COOKED) 5-6 SERVINGS
GRANULATED SUGAR	8 OZ	1 POUND	1 1/2 POUNDS
WATER	1 TBSP	2 TBSP	3 TBSP

INGREDIENTS FOR THE FLAN MIXTURE

EVAPORATED MILK	1/3 CUP	2/3 CUP	1 CUP
SWEETENED CONDENSED MILK	1/3 CUP	2/3 CUP	1 CUP
EGG YOLKS, LARGE	2	4	6
VANILLA EXTRACT	1/4 tsp	1/2 tsp	3/4 tsp

Method:

1. *In a microwave-safe glass measuring cup, stir together the sugar and water until moistened.*
2. *Microwave for 1-2 minutes or until bubbly and mixture turns amber in color.*
3. *Pour sugar into a 1-cup size ramekin or glass bowl that will fit inside the rice cooker.*
4. *Using potholders, swirl caramel inside the ramekin to coat bottom and sides; set aside.*
5. *In a small mixing bowl, whisk together the flan mixture ingredients.*
6. *Pour mixture into the caramel-lined ramekin and cover tightly with aluminum foil.*
7. *Place a folded paper towel into the bottom of the rice cooker.*
8. *Create a water bath by pouring 1/3 cup water over the paper towel then carefully lower the ramekin into the rice cooker.*
9. *Close lid and press COOK.*
10. *Cook for 20-25 minutes or until a knife inserted into the flan off-center comes out clean.*
11. *When cooking is complete, chill flan for 1 hour or up to 3 days.*
12. *When ready to serve, run a thin knife around the edge of the ramekin to loosen the flan.*
13. *Invert onto a small, lipped serving dish and allow the now liquid caramel to flow over the flan.*
14. *Garnish as desired and serve.*

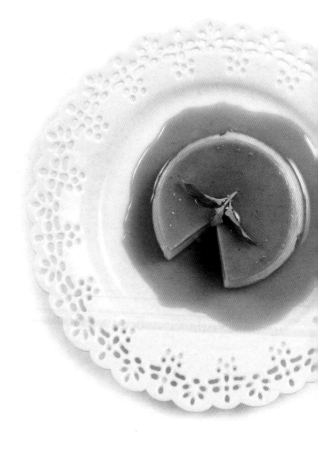

HARD BOILED
EGGS

	1.5 CUP (3 CUPS COOKED) 1-2 SERVINGS	3 CUP (6 CUPS COOKED) 3-4 SERVINGS	5 CUP (10 CUPS COOKED) 5-6 SERVINGS
REFRIGERATED LARGE EGGS	1-4	4-8	8-12
WATER AT ROOM TEMPERATURE	1 1/2 CUPS	3 CUPS	4 1/2 CUPS

Method:

1. *Place eggs in the rice cooker then add enough water to cover the eggs inside the rice cooker.*
2. *Close lid and press COOK.*
3. *Set a kitchen timer for 20 minutes.*
4. *When timer rings, drain off the water using a potholder.*
5. *Shake the rice cooker insert back and forth to crack the eggs all over.*
6. *Run cold water over the eggs and peel starting at the fat end of the eggs. Let a stream of cold water flow over the eggs while peeling as it will help in removing the shell.*
7. *Use eggs as desired. Eggs can be stored in the refrigerator for up to 7 days.*

TIP

For soft boiled eggs, set the timer for 15 minutes and be more gentle with cracking and peeling since the yolk inside is runny.

EASY
MEATLOAF

	1.5 CUP (3 CUPS COOKED) 1-2 SERVINGS	3 CUP (6 CUPS COOKED) 3-4 SERVINGS	5 CUP (10 CUPS COOKED) 5-6 SERVINGS
LEAN GROUND BEEF, RAW	8 OZ	1 POUND	1 1/2 POUNDS
YELLOW ONIONS, CHOPPED	2 TBSP	1/4 CUP	1/3 CUP
LARGE EGGS	1	2	3
YELLOW MUSTARD	1 TBSP	2 TBSP	3 TBSP
SLICED BREAD, TORN INTO SMALL PIECES	1 SLICE	2 SLICES	3 SLICES
WHOLE MILK	1 TBSP	2 TBSP	3 TBSP
KOSHER SALT AND FRESHLY GROUND PEPPER	TO TASTE	TO TASTE	TO TASTE
WORCESTERSHIRE SAUCE	1 tsp	2 tsp	1 TBSP
GROUND SAGE	1/4 tsp	1/2 tsp	3/4 tsp
KETCHUP	1/4 CUP	1/2 CUP	3/4 CUP
FRENCH FRIED ONIONS, STORE-BOUGHT	1/2 CUP	1 CUP	1 1/2 CUPS

Method:

1. *In a mixing bowl, blend together all ingredients, except French fried onions.*
2. *Spoon mixture into the rice cooker then smooth the top.*
3. *Close lid and press COOK.*
4. *Cook for 40-45 minutes or until the meatloaf is cooked through (165°F on a meat thermometer).*
5. *When cooking is complete, top with French fried onions, garnish as desired and serve.*

TIP

Serve with Garlic Mashed Potatoes (see page 66) and Honey Glazed Carrots (see page 69).

CHICKEN
LETTUCE WRAPS

	1.5 CUP (3 CUPS COOKED) 1-2 SERVINGS	3 CUP (6 CUPS COOKED) 3-4 SERVINGS	5 CUP (10 CUPS COOKED) 5-6 SERVINGS
DARK SESAME OIL	1 TBSP	2 TBSP	3 TBSP
GROUND CHICKEN, UNCOOKED	8 OZ	1 POUND	1 1/2 POUNDS
CHICKEN STOCK	3 TBSP	1/4 CUP + 2 TBSP	1/2 CUP + 1 TBSP
CORNSTARCH	1 TBSP	2 TBSP	3 TBSP
GARLIC CLOVES, CHOPPED	3	6	9
FRESH GINGER, CHOPPED	1 tsp	2 tsp	1 TBSP
YELLOW ONIONS, CHOPPED	2 TBSP	1/4 CUP	1/3 CUP
BUTTON MUSHROOMS, CHOPPED	4	8	12
GREEN ONIONS, CHOPPED	2	4	6
WATER CHESTNUTS, DICED	1/4 CUP	1/2 CUP	3/4 CUP
SOY SAUCE	TO TASTE	TO TASTE	TO TASTE
BUTTER LETTUCE OR ICEBERG LETTUCE FOR SERVING	AS DESIRED	AS DESIRED	AS DESIRED

Method:

1. Combine all ingredients, except lettuce, in the rice cooker and stir thoroughly.
2. Close lid and press COOK.
3. Cook for 20 minutes or until chicken is cooked through and mixture is thick and bubbly, stirring occasionally.
4. Wrap in lettuce leaves, garnish as desired and serve.

TIP
Serve this with the Perfect White Rice on page 11.

ONE POT
PASTA

	1.5 CUP (3 CUPS COOKED) 1-2 SERVINGS	3 CUP (6 CUPS COOKED) 3-4 SERVINGS	5 CUP (10 CUPS COOKED) 5-6 SERVINGS
LEAN GROUND TURKEY, RAW	8 OZ	1 POUND	1 1/2 POUNDS
SMALL SIZE PASTA, UNCOOKED	1/2 CUP	1 CUP	1 1/2 CUPS
CHICKEN STOCK	1/2 CUP	1 CUP	1 1/2 CUPS
PASTA SAUCE, JARRED	1/4 CUP	1/2 CUP	3/4 CUP
ITALIAN DRESSING, STORE-BOUGHT	1 TBSP	2 TBSP	3 TBSP
WHITE WINE	2 TBSP	1/4 CUP	1/3 CUP
PARMESAN CHEESE, GRATED	1/4 CUP	1/2 CUP	3/4 CUP
KOSHER SALT AND FRESHLY GROUND PEPPER	TO TASTE	TO TASTE	TO TASTE
FRESH SPINACH LEAVES	1 CUP	2 CUPS	3 CUPS

Method:

1. *Combine all ingredients in the rice cooker; stir to break up the turkey.*
2. *Close lid and press COOK.*
3. *Cook for 20-25 minutes or until pasta is tender.*
4. *When cooking is complete, garnish as desired and serve.*

TIP
For brighter colored spinach, add it during the last 5 minutes of cooking.

BEEF & BROCCOLI
RICE

	1.5 CUP (3 CUPS COOKED) 1-2 SERVINGS	3 CUP (6 CUPS COOKED) 3-4 SERVINGS	5 CUP (10 CUPS COOKED) 5-6 SERVINGS
BASMATI WHITE RICE, UNCOOKED	1/2 CUP	1 CUP	1 1/2 CUPS
BEEF STOCK	1/2 CUP	1 CUP	1 1/2 CUPS
OLIVE OIL	1 TBSP	2 TBSP	3 TBSP
BEEF SIRLOIN, RAW, THINLY SLICED	4 OZ	8 OZ	12 OZ
YELLOW ONIONS, SLICED	2 TBSP	1/4 CUP	1/3 CUP
GARLIC CLOVES, CHOPPED	2	4	6
FRESH GINGER, CHOPPED	1 TBSP	2 TBSP	3 TBSP
SMALL CARROT, SLICED	1	2	3
SOY SAUCE	TO TASTE	TO TASTE	TO TASTE
FRESH BROCCOLI FLORETS	1/2 CUP	1 CUP	1 1/2 CUPS

Method:

1. *Combine all ingredients, except broccoli, in the rice cooker and stir.*
2. *Close lid and press COOK.*
3. *After 15 minutes of cooking, add the broccoli and continue to cook for an additional 5-10 minutes or until rice and beef are tender and sauce is thick and bubbly.*
4. *When cooking is complete, garnish as desired and serve.*

PIZZA
CASSEROLE

	1.5 CUP (3 CUPS COOKED) 1-2 SERVINGS	3 CUP (6 CUPS COOKED) 3-4 SERVINGS	5 CUP (10 CUPS COOKED) 5-6 SERVINGS
PIZZA-FLAVORED CRACKERS	1/2 CUP	1 CUP	1 1/2 CUPS
PEPPERONI SLICES	1/4 CUP	1/2 CUP	3/4 CUP
PASTA SAUCE, JARRED	1/2 CUP	1 CUP	1 1/2 CUPS
CHICKEN STOCK	1/4 CUP	1/2 CUP	3/4 CUP
GARLIC CLOVES, CHOPPED	2	4	6
KOSHER SALT AND FRESHLY GROUND PEPPER	TO TASTE	TO TASTE	TO TASTE
ITALIAN DRESSING, STORE-BOUGHT	1 TBSP	2 TBSP	3 TBSP
PARMESAN CHEESE, GRATED	2 TBSP	1/4 CUP	1/3 CUP
MOZZARELLA CHEESE, SHREDDED	1/4 CUP	1/2 CUP	3/4 CUP

Method:

1. Combine all ingredients, except mozzarella cheese, in the rice cooker and stir well.
2. Close lid and press COOK.
3. Cook for 20-25 minutes or until hot and bubbly.
4. When cooking is complete, top with mozzarella and close lid again.
5. Let rest on WARM for 5 minutes or until cheese is melted.
6. Garnish as desired and serve.

TIP

If you prefer sausage, ham, pineapple or other pizza toppings, just add them to the rice cooker before cooking. Make sure you don't exceed the MAX line of your rice cooker insert.

BAKED PEPPERONI
ZITI

	1.5 CUP (3 CUPS COOKED) 1-2 SERVINGS	3 CUP (6 CUPS COOKED) 3-4 SERVINGS	5 CUP (10 CUPS COOKED) 5-6 SERVINGS
PASTA SAUCE, JARRED	1/2 CUP	1 CUP	1 1/2 CUPS
ZITI PASTA, UNCOOKED	1/2 CUP	1 CUP	1 1/2 CUPS
KOSHER SALT AND FRESHLY GROUND PEPPER	TO TASTE	TO TASTE	TO TASTE
PEPPERONI SLICES	2 OZ	4 OZ	6 OZ
WATER	1/4 CUP	1/2 CUP	3/4 CUP
PARMESAN CHEESE, GRATED	1/4 CUP	1/2 CUP	3/4 CUP
PARSLEY, CHOPPED, FOR SERVING	AS DESIRED	AS DESIRED	AS DESIRED

Method:

1. *Combine all ingredients, except parsley, in the rice cooker and stir.*
2. *Close lid and press COOK.*
3. *Cook for 20-25 minutes or until pasta is tender and sauce is thick and bubbly.*
4. *When cooking is complete, sprinkle with parsley, garnish as desired and serve.*

BANANAS FOSTER
BREAD PUDDING

	1.5 CUP (3 CUPS COOKED) 1-2 SERVINGS	3 CUP (6 CUPS COOKED) 3-4 SERVINGS	5 CUP (10 CUPS COOKED) 5-6 SERVINGS
UNSALTED BUTTER, MELTED	1 TBSP	2 TBSP	3 TBSP
LIGHT BROWN SUGAR, PACKED	2 TBSP	1/4 CUP	1/3 CUP
BANANA LIQUEUR	1 TBSP	2 TBSP	3 TBSP
BANANA, SLICED	1	2	3
HEAVY CREAM	1/3 CUP	2/3 CUP	1 CUP
LARGE EGG	1	2	3
BAGUETTE SLICES, TORN	3	6	9
ICE CREAM AND BOTTLED CARAMEL FOR SERVING	AS DESIRED	AS DESIRED	AS DESIRED

Method:

1. Place butter, sugar, liqueur and banana into the rice cooker; stir.
2. In a bowl, stir together the cream, egg and baguette slices.
3. Pour the egg mixture over the banana mixture in the rice cooker but do not stir.
4. Close lid and press COOK.
5. Cook for 20-25 minutes or until mixture is set (it should jiggle and not be shiny on top when it is done and a knife inserted off-center should come out clean).
6. Top with ice cream and caramel sauce.
7. Garnish as desired and serve.

BANANA
BREAD

	1.5 CUP (3 CUPS COOKED) 1-2 SERVINGS	3 CUP (6 CUPS COOKED) 3-4 SERVINGS	5 CUP (10 CUPS COOKED) 5-6 SERVINGS
RIPE BANANA, MASHED	1	2	3
UNSALTED BUTTER, MELTED	2 TBSP	1/4 CUP	1/3 CUP
LARGE EGG, BEATEN	1	2	3
GRANULATED SUGAR	1/4 CUP	1/2 CUP	3/4 CUP
BAKING SODA	1/4 tsp	1/2 tsp	3/4 tsp
ALL PURPOSE FLOUR	1/2 CUP	1 CUP	1 1/2 CUPS
KOSHER SALT	1 PINCH	2 PINCHES	3 PINCHES

Method:

1. *Apply nonstick cooking spray to the rice cooker.*
2. *In a bowl, whisk together all ingredients then pour into the rice cooker.*
3. *Close lid and press COOK.*
4. *When rice cooker switches to WARM (about 6-7 minutes), wait for 5-6 minutes then press COOK again; repeat if necessary until cooking is complete.*
5. *Cooking is complete after about 20-25 minutes of cooking or when the top of the bread is pale and dull looking and a wooden pick inserted slightly off-center comes out with just a few moist crumbs clinging to it.*
6. *When done, invert onto a small serving plate so that the brown part is on top.*
7. *Garnish as desired and serve.*

TIP

Instead of throwing away over-ripe bananas, freeze them instead and use them in dishes like this. You can microwave them to thaw before using.

APPLE CRUMBLE

	1.5 CUP (3 CUPS COOKED) 1-2 SERVINGS	3 CUP (6 CUPS COOKED) 3-4 SERVINGS	5 CUP (10 CUPS COOKED) 5-6 SERVINGS
MEDIUM APPLES, SLICED	2	4	6
WATER	2 TBSP	1/4 CUP	2/3 CUP
LIGHT BROWN SUGAR, PACKED	1/4 CUP	1/2 CUP	3/4 CUP
GROUND CINNAMON	1 tsp	2 tsp	3 tsp
UNSALTED BUTTER	2 TBSP	1/4 CUP	1/3 CUP
ALL PURPOSE FLOUR	1 TBSP	2 TBSP	3 TBSP
KOSHER SALT	PINCH	2 PINCHES	3 PINCHES
GRANOLA, STORE-BOUGHT	1/2 CUP	1 CUP	1 1/2 CUPS

Method:

1. Combine all ingredients, except granola, in the rice cooker.
2. Close lid and press COOK.
3. Cook for 30 minutes or until apples are soft and sauce is thick and bubbly, stirring occasionally.
4. If rice cooker switches to WARM during the 30 minutes cooking, wait for 5-6 minutes then press COOK again; repeat if necessary.
5. When cooking is complete, spoon into serving dishes.
6. Top with granola, garnish as desired and serve.

BACON SCALLOPED
POTATOES

	1.5 CUP (3 CUPS COOKED) 1-2 SERVINGS	3 CUP (6 CUPS COOKED) 3-4 SERVINGS	5 CUP (10 CUPS COOKED) 5-6 SERVINGS
SMALL RUSSET POTATO, SLICED	2	4	6
GREEN ONION, SLICED	1	2	3
HEAVY CREAM	1/2 CUP	1 CUP	1 1/2 CUPS
BACON SLICES, CHOPPED	2	4	6
KOSHER SALT	TO TASTE	TO TASTE	TO TASTE

Method:

1. *Combine all ingredients in the rice cooker.*
2. *Close lid and press COOK.*
3. *Cook for 20-25 minutes or until potatoes are tender and sauce is bubbly.*
4. *When cooking is complete, garnish as desired and serve.*

EGGPLANT & SAUSAGE
LASAGNA

	1.5 CUP (3 CUPS COOKED) 1-2 SERVINGS	3 CUP (6 CUPS COOKED) 3-4 SERVINGS	5 CUP (10 CUPS COOKED) 5-6 SERVINGS
SMALL EGGPLANT, THINLY SLICED	1	2	3
OLIVE OIL	2 TBSP	1/4 CUP	1/3 CUP
KOSHER SALT AND FRESHLY GROUND PEPPER	TO TASTE	TO TASTE	TO TASTE
SAUSAGE CRUMBLES, COOKED	1/2 CUP	1 CUP	1 1/2 CUPS
PASTA SAUCE, JARRED	1/2 CUP	1 CUP	1 1/2 CUPS
LARGE EGG	1	2	3
RICOTTA CHEESE	1/4 CUP	1/2 CUP	3/4 CUP
PARMESAN CHEESE, GRATED	1/4 CUP	1/2 CUP	3/4 CUP
MOZZARELLA CHEESE, SHREDDED	1/4 CUP	1/2 CUP	3/4 CUP

Method:

1. *Place eggplant slices on a sheet pan then season with olive oil, salt and pepper.*
2. *In a mixing bowl, combine remaining ingredients.*
3. *Place 2 eggplant slices in the bottom of the rice cooker.*
4. *Top eggplant slices with a third of the meat mixture then stack by adding two additional eggplant slices and another third of the meat mixture.*
5. *Repeat to make a third layer, making sure that you do not stack higher than the rice cooker insert MAX line (you may have extra eggplant slices leftover).*
6. *Close lid and press COOK.*
7. *Cook for 1 hour or until eggplant is tender.*
8. *When cooking is complete, carefully transfer the lasagna to a serving bowl or plate.*
9. *Garnish as desired and serve.*

CHICKEN
BURRITO

	1.5 CUP (3 CUPS COOKED) 1-2 SERVINGS	3 CUP (6 CUPS COOKED) 3-4 SERVINGS	5 CUP (10 CUPS COOKED) 5-6 SERVINGS
CHICKEN TENDERS, RAW, DICED	3	6	9
TACO SEASONING	TO TASTE	TO TASTE	TO TASTE
CORN KERNELS, FROZEN	1/4 CUP	1/2 CUP	3/4 CUP
CANNED TOMATOES WITH GREEN CHILIES (11 OZ SIZE)	1 CAN	2 CANS	3 CANS
MEXICAN BLEND CHEESE, SHREDDED	1/2 CUP	1 CUP	1 1/2 CUPS
BLACK BEANS, CANNED, DRAINED AND RINSED	1/2 CUP	1 CUP	1 1/2 CUPS
FRESH CILANTRO, SOUR CREAM AND TORTILLAS FOR SERVING	AS DESIRED	AS DESIRED	AS DESIRED

Method:

1. *Combine all ingredients, except cilantro, sour cream and tortillas, in the rice cooker.*
2. *Stir well then close lid and press COOK.*
3. *Cook for 20-25 minutes or until chicken is cooked through.*
4. *Garnish as desired and serve with cilantro, sour cream and tortillas.*

BRUSSELS SPROUTS
WITH BACON

	1.5 CUP (3 CUPS COOKED) 1-2 SERVINGS	3 CUP (6 CUPS COOKED) 3-4 SERVINGS	5 CUP (10 CUPS COOKED) 5-6 SERVINGS
BACON SLICES, RAW, CHOPPED	3	6	9
RED ONIONS, CHOPPED	1 TBSP	2 TBSP	3 TBSP
APPLE CIDER VINEGAR	1 TBSP	2 TBSP	3 TBSP
HONEY	1 TBSP	2 TBSP	3 TBSP
KOSHER SALT AND FRESHLY GROUND PEPPER	TO TASTE	TO TASTE	TO TASTE
BRUSSELS SPROUTS, HALVED	1 1/2 CUPS	3 CUPS	4 1/2 CUPS

Method:

1. Combine all ingredients in the rice cooker and stir.
2. Close lid and press COOK.
3. Cook for 15 minutes or until just crisp tender.
4. When cooking is complete, garnish as desired and serve.

TIP
Turkey bacon is delicious in this recipe as well if you're trying to save calories.

CAULIFLOWER WITH CHEESE SAUCE

	1.5 CUP (3 CUPS COOKED) 1-2 SERVINGS	3 CUP (6 CUPS COOKED) 3-4 SERVINGS	5 CUP (10 CUPS COOKED) 5-6 SERVINGS
UNSALTED BUTTER	1 TBSP	2 TBSP	3 TBSP
ALL PURPOSE FLOUR	1 TBSP	2 TBSP	3 TBSP
WHOLE MILK	1/3 CUP	2/3 CUP	1 CUP
KOSHER SALT AND FRESHLY GROUND PEPPER	TO TASTE	TO TASTE	TO TASTE
HOT PEPPER SAUCE, BOTTLED (OPTIONAL)	1/2 tsp	1 tsp	1 1/2 tsp
FRESH CAULIFLOWER FLORETS	1 1/2 CUPS	3 CUPS	4 1/2 CUPS
EXTRA SHARP CHEDDAR CHEESE, SHREDDED	1/3 CUP	2/3 CUP	1 CUP

Method:

1. *Combine all ingredients in the rice cooker and stir.*
2. *Close lid and press COOK.*
3. *Cook for 20 minutes or until cauliflower is tender and sauce is thick and bubbly, stirring occasionally.*
4. *When cooking is complete, garnish as desired and serve.*

BEEF & BARLEY
STEW

	1.5 CUP (3 CUPS COOKED) 1-2 SERVINGS	3 CUP (6 CUPS COOKED) 3-4 SERVINGS	5 CUP (10 CUPS COOKED) 5-6 SERVINGS
PEARL BARLEY	1/2 CUP	1 CUP	1 1/2 CUPS
BEEF STEW PIECES, RAW, THINLY SLICED	4 OZ	8 OZ	12 OZ
SMALL YELLOW ONION, CHOPPED	1/4 CUP	1/2 CUP	3/4 CUP
CELERY, CHOPPED	2 TBSP	4 TBSP	6 TBSP
CARROT, CHOPPED	1/4 CUP	1/2 CUP	3/4 CUP
BEEF STOCK	1 CUP	2 CUPS	3 CUPS
KETCHUP	1 TBSP	2 TBSP	3 TBSP
KOSHER SALT AND FRESHLY GROUND PEPPER	TO TASTE	TO TASTE	TO TASTE

Method:

1. Combine all ingredients in the rice cooker and stir.
2. Close lid and press COOK.
3. Cook for 30 minutes or until thick and beef is tender.
4. When cooking is complete, garnish as desired and serve.

BREAD PUDDING WITH
SALTED CARAMEL

	1.5 CUP (3 CUPS COOKED) 1-2 SERVINGS	3 CUP (6 CUPS COOKED) 3-4 SERVINGS	5 CUP (10 CUPS COOKED) 5-6 SERVINGS
CHOCOLATE CHIPS	1/4 CUP	1/2 CUP	3/4 CUP
HEAVY CREAM	3/4 CUP	1 1/2 CUPS	2 1/4 CUPS
LIGHT BROWN SUGAR, PACKED	2 TBSP	1/4 CUP	1/3 CUP
LARGE EGGS, BEATEN	2	4	6
KOSHER SALT, PLUS MORE FOR SPRINKLING	PINCH	2 PINCHES	3 PINCHES
LEMON JUICE	1/2 tsp	1 tsp	1 1/2 tsp
ITALIAN BREAD SLICES, TORN	2	4	6
JARRED CARAMEL SAUCE, FOR SERVING	1/4 CUP	1/2 CUP	3/4 CUP

Method:

1. *Combine all ingredients, except caramel sauce, in the rice cooker and stir thoroughly.*
2. *Close lid and press COOK.*
3. *When rice cooker switches to WARM (about 6-7 minutes), wait for 5-6 minutes then press COOK again; repeat if necessary until cooking is complete.*
4. *Cooking is complete after about 20-25 minutes of cooking or when a knife inserted slightly off-center comes out clean.*
5. *When done, invert onto small serving plate and drizzle with caramel sauce.*
6. *Sprinkle lightly with additional kosher salt, garnish as desired and serve.*

SLOPPY CHEESEBURGERS

	1.5 CUP (3 CUPS COOKED) 1-2 SERVINGS	3 CUP (6 CUPS COOKED) 3-4 SERVINGS	5 CUP (10 CUPS COOKED) 5-6 SERVINGS
LEAN GROUND BEEF, RAW	8 OZ	1 POUND	1 1/2 POUNDS
BEEF STOCK	2 TBSP	1/4 CUP	1/3 CUP
YELLOW ONION, CHOPPED	1/4 CUP	1/2 CUP	3/4 CUP
KOSHER SALT AND FRESHLY GROUND PEPPER	TO TASTE	TO TASTE	TO TASTE
DILL PICKLE RELISH	1 TBSP	2 TBSP	3 TBSP
KETCHUP	1/4 CUP	1/2 CUP	3/4 CUP
YELLOW MUSTARD	1 TBSP	2 TBSP	3 TBSP
AMERICAN CHEESE SLICES	2	4	6
HAMBURGER BUNS	1-2	3-4	5-6

Method:

1. *Combine all ingredients, except cheese and buns, in the rice cooker and stir.*
2. *Close lid and press COOK.*
3. *Cook for 20 minutes or until beef is cooked through, stirring occasionally.*
4. *Add the cheese and stir until melted.*
5. *Spoon onto buns, garnish as desired and serve.*

CHEESY BROCCOLI & RICE

	1.5 CUP (3 CUPS COOKED) 1-2 SERVINGS	3 CUP (6 CUPS COOKED) 3-4 SERVINGS	5 CUP (10 CUPS COOKED) 5-6 SERVINGS
UNSALTED BUTTER	1 TBSP	2 TBSP	3 TBSP
YELLOW ONION, CHOPPED	2 TBSP	1/4 CUP	1/3 CUP
BROCCOLI FLORETS, FRESH OR FROZEN	1 1/2 CUPS	3 CUPS	4 1/2 CUPS
KOSHER SALT AND FRESHLY GROUND PEPPER	TO TASTE	TO TASTE	TO TASTE
MILK OR WATER	1/4 CUP	1/2 CUP	3/4 CUP
HOT PEPPER SAUCE, BOTTLED (OPTIONAL)	1/2 tsp	1 tsp	1 1/2 tsp
SHARP CHEDDAR CHEESE, SHREDDED	1/3 CUP	2/3 CUP	1 CUP
PERFECT WHITE RICE, COOKED (SEE PAGE 11)	1/4 CUP	1/2 CUP	3/4 CUP

Method:

1. *Combine all ingredients in the rice cooker and stir.*
2. *Close lid and press COOK.*
3. *Cook for 20 minutes or until thick and bubbly.*
4. *Spoon into serving bowls, garnish as desired and serve.*

CHICKEN FETTUCCINE
ALFREDO

	1.5 CUP (3 CUPS COOKED) 1-2 SERVINGS	3 CUP (6 CUPS COOKED) 3-4 SERVINGS	5 CUP (10 CUPS COOKED) 5-6 SERVINGS
CHICKEN TENDERS, RAW, DICED	3	6	9
FETTUCCINE NOODLES, BROKEN, UNCOOKED	1/2 CUP	1 CUP	1 1/2 CUPS
HALF & HALF	2/3 CUP	1 1/3 CUPS	2 CUPS
PARMESAN CHEESE, GRATED	1/4 CUP	1/2 CUP	3/4 CUP
CHICKEN-FLAVORED BASE, STORE-BOUGHT	1 tsp	2 tsp	1 TBSP
WHITE WINE	1 TBSP	2 TBSP	3 TBSP
GARLIC CLOVES, CHOPPED	4	8	12
CHILI FLAKES (OPTIONAL)	PINCH	2 PINCHES	3 PINCHES
KOSHER SALT AND FRESHLY GROUND PEPPER	TO TASTE	TO TASTE	TO TASTE
CHOPPED PARSLEY FOR SERVING	AS DESIRED	AS DESIRED	AS DESIRED

Method:

1. Combine all ingredients, except parsley, in the rice cooker and stir.
2. Close lid and press COOK.
3. Cook for 20-25 minutes or until noodles are tender, stirring occasionally.
4. Pour into a serving dish and top with parsley.
5. Garnish as desired and serve.

CHICKEN & DUMPLINGS
FOR ONE

	1.5 CUP (3 CUPS COOKED) 1-2 SERVINGS	3 CUP (6 CUPS COOKED) 3-4 SERVINGS	5 CUP (10 CUPS COOKED) 5-6 SERVINGS
CHICKEN TENDERS, RAW, DICED	3	6	9
KOSHER SALT AND FRESHLY GROUND PEPPER	TO TASTE	TO TASTE	TO TASTE
CHICKEN-FLAVORED BASE, STORE-BOUGHT	1 TBSP	2 TBSP	3 TBSP
WHOLE MILK	1/2 CUP	1 CUP	1 1/2 CUPS
ALL PURPOSE FLOUR	1 TBSP	2 TBSP	3 TBSP
DRIED SAGE	1/4 tsp	1/2 tsp	3/4 tsp
CELERY, DICED	2 TBSP	1/4 CUP	1/3 CUP
YELLOW ONION, DICED	2 TBSP	1/4 CUP	1/3 CUP
FROZEN PEAS & CARROTS MIX	1/4 CUP	1/2 CUP	3/4 CUP
REFRIGERATED BISCUITS FROM A MINI CAN, HALVED	2	4	6

Method:

1. *Combine all ingredients, except biscuits, in the rice cooker and stir.*
2. *Close lid and press COOK.*
3. *Cook for 20 minutes or until thick and bubbly.*
4. *Roll biscuits into 4 balls and place on top of the chicken mixture.*
5. *Close lid and cook for 5 minutes or until biscuits are puffed.*
6. *Garnish as desired and serve.*

TIP
You can use frozen chicken tenders and even dice them while frozen if you have a sturdy knife.

RICE COOKER RECIPES

49

CORN CAKE

	1.5 CUP (3 CUPS COOKED) 1-2 SERVINGS	3 CUP (6 CUPS COOKED) 3-4 SERVINGS	5 CUP (10 CUPS COOKED) 5-6 SERVINGS
CREAMED CORN, CANNED IS FINE	1/4 CUP	1/2 CUP	3/4 CUP
UNSALTED BUTTER, MELTED	1/4 CUP	1/2 CUP	3/4 CUP
LARGE EGGS	2	4	6
YELLOW CORNMEAL	1/4 CUP	1/2 CUP	3/4 CUP
ALL PURPOSE FLOUR	1/4 CUP	1/2 CUP	3/4 CUP
GRANULATED SUGAR	2 TBSP	1/4 CUP	1/3 CUP
BAKING POWDER	3/4 tsp	1 1/2 tsp	2 1/4 tsp
KOSHER SALT	1/4 tsp	1/2 tsp	3/4 tsp
BUTTER AND HONEY FOR SERVING	AS DESIRED	AS DESIRED	AS DESIRED

Method:

1. *Apply nonstick cooking spray to rice cooker.*
2. *In a small mixing bowl, combine all ingredients, except butter and honey for serving; stir until semi smooth.*
3. *Pour mixture into the rice cooker, close lid and press COOK.*
4. *When rice cooker switches to WARM (about 6-7 minutes), wait for 5-6 minutes then press COOK again; repeat 1-2 additional times or until the top of the cornbread is opaque with no shiny batter at the center (insert a wooden pick slightly off-center to test for doneness, it should come out with just a few moist crumbs clinging to it).*
5. *Invert corn cake onto small serving plate and serve with butter and honey.*

CREAM OF WHEAT
WITH PECANS

	1.5 CUP (3 CUPS COOKED) 1-2 SERVINGS	3 CUP (6 CUPS COOKED) 3-4 SERVINGS	5 CUP (10 CUPS COOKED) 5-6 SERVINGS
WHOLE MILK	1/4 CUP	1/2 CUP	3/4 CUP
WATER	1 CUP	2 CUPS	3 CUPS
UNSALTED BUTTER	1 TBSP	2 TBSP	3 TBSP
CREAM OF WHEAT CEREAL	3 TBSP	1/4 CUP + 2 TBSP	1/2 CUP + 1 TBSP
KOSHER SALT	PINCH	2 PINCHES	3 PINCHES
MAPLE SYRUP	2 TBSP	1/4 CUP	1/3 CUP
PECAN PIECES, TOASTED	2 TBSP	1/4 CUP	1/3 CUP
ADDITIONAL SYRUP FOR SERVING	AS DESIRED	AS DESIRED	AS DESIRED

Method:

1. *Combine all ingredients, except syrup for serving, in the rice cooker and stir.*
2. *Close lid and press COOK.*
3. *Cook for 15-20 minutes or until thick and bubbly, stirring occasionally using a potholder.*
4. *When cooking is complete, serve in bowls topped with additional syrup.*
5. *Garnish as desired and serve.*

CHEESY CHICKEN & NOODLES

	1.5 CUP (3 CUPS COOKED) 1-2 SERVINGS	3 CUP (6 CUPS COOKED) 3-4 SERVINGS	5 CUP (10 CUPS COOKED) 5-6 SERVINGS
CHICKEN TENDERS, RAW	3	6	9
SMALL PASTA, UNCOOKED	1/2 CUP	1 CUP	1 1/2 CUPS
WHOLE MILK	1/2 CUP	1 CUP	1 1/2 CUPS
ALL PURPOSE FLOUR	1 TBSP	2 TBSP	3 TBSP
KOSHER SALT AND FRESHLY GROUND PEPPER	TO TASTE	TO TASTE	TO TASTE
YELLOW ONIONS, CHOPPED	2 TBSP	1/4 CUP	1/3 CUP
YELLOW MUSTARD	2 tsp	4 tsp	2 TBSP
FROZEN PEAS & CARROTS MIX	1/4 CUP	1/2 CUP	3/4 CUP
SHARP CHEDDAR CHEESE, SHREDDED	1/4 CUP	1/2 CUP	3/4 CUP
CHEESY CRACKERS, CRUSHED	1/4 CUP	1/2 CUP	3/4 CUP

Method:

1. *Combine all ingredients, except cheese and crackers, in the rice cooker and stir.*
2. *Close lid and press COOK.*
3. *Cook for 20-25 minutes or until pasta is tender, chicken is cooked through and the sauce is thick.*
4. *Stir in the cheese until melted.*
5. *Top with cheesy crackers, garnish as desired and serve.*

TIP
This dish is great with leftover rotisserie chicken.

CHEESY GARLIC
PULL APART ROLLS

	1.5 CUP (3 CUPS COOKED) 1-2 SERVINGS	3 CUP (6 CUPS COOKED) 3-4 SERVINGS	5 CUP (10 CUPS COOKED) 5-6 SERVINGS
UNSALTED BUTTER, MELTED	2 TBSP	1/4 CUP	1/3 CUP
GARLIC POWDER	1/2 tsp	1 tsp	1 1/2 tsp
KOSHER SALT	1/4 tsp	1/2 tsp	3/4 tsp
PARMESAN CHEESE, GRATED	1 TBSP	2 TBSP	3 TBSP
SHARP CHEDDAR CHEESE, GRATED	1 TBSP	2 TBSP	3 TBSP
FROZEN DINNER ROLL DOUGH BALLS, RAW (GOLF BALL SIZE)	6	12	18

Method:

1. *Apply nonstick cooking spray to the rice cooker and keep the unit unplugged.*
2. *In a small mixing bowl combine the butter, garlic and salt.*
3. *Pour half of the butter mixture into the rice cooker.*
4. *Sprinkle half of the cheeses over the butter mixture then top with dough balls.*
5. *Drizzle with remaining butter mixture and top with remaining cheeses.*
6. *Close lid and let rest for 40 minutes or until puffed (keep unit unplugged).*
7. *After 40 minutes, plug in the rice cooker and press COOK.*
8. *When rice cooker switches to WARM (about 6-7 minutes), let rest for 5-6 minutes then press COOK again.*
9. *When rice cooker switches to WARM again, set a kitchen timer for 15 minutes.*
10. *After 15 minutes press tops, they should spring back and be dull tan in color; cook for a few more minutes if needed.*
11. *Invert onto a small serving plate so that the brown part is on top.*
12. *Garnish as desired and serve.*

BROCCOLI WITH
BACON & RAISINS

	1.5 CUP (3 CUPS COOKED) 1-2 SERVINGS	3 CUP (6 CUPS COOKED) 3-4 SERVINGS	5 CUP (10 CUPS COOKED) 5-6 SERVINGS
RED ONIONS, DICED	2 TBSP	1/4 CUP	1/3 CUP
DARK RAISINS	2 TBSP	1/4 CUP	1/3 CUP
COOKED BACON STRIPS, CRUMBLED	2	4	6
OLIVE OIL	1 TBSP	2 TBSP	3 TBSP
GRANULATED SUGAR	1 TBSP	2 TBSP	3 TBSP
APPLE CIDER VINEGAR	1 TBSP	2 TBSP	3 TBSP
KOSHER SALT AND FRESHLY GROUND PEPPER	TO TASTE	TO TASTE	TO TASTE
BROCCOLI FLORETS	1 1/2 CUPS	3 CUPS	4 1/2 CUPS

Method:

1. *Combine all ingredients in the rice cooker and stir.*
2. *Close lid and press COOK.*
3. *Cook for 7-10 minutes or until broccoli is crisp tender.*
4. *Garnish as desired and serve.*

BROWNIE
PUDDING CAKE

	1.5 CUP (3 CUPS COOKED) 1-2 SERVINGS	3 CUP (6 CUPS COOKED) 3-4 SERVINGS	5 CUP (10 CUPS COOKED) 5-6 SERVINGS
CANOLA OIL	3 TBSP	1/4 CUP + 2 TBSP	1/2 CUP + 1 TBSP
LARGE EGG, BEATEN	1	2	3
WHOLE MILK OR ALMOND MILK	3 TBSP	1/4 CUP + 2 TBSP	1/2 CUP + 1 TBSP
VANILLA EXTRACT	1/4 tsp	1/2 tsp	3/4 tsp
ALL PURPOSE FLOUR	3 TBSP	1/4 CUP + 2 TBSP	1/2 CUP + 1 TBSP
GRANULATED SUGAR	1/4 CUP	1/2 CUP	3/4 CUP
KOSHER SALT	1/4 tsp	1/2 tsp	3/4 tsp
COCOA POWDER	2 TBSP	1/4 CUP	1/4 CUP + 2 TBSP
CHOCOLATE CHIPS	3 TBSP	1/4 CUP + 2 TBSP	1/2 CUP + 1 TBSP

Method:

1. *Combine all ingredients in the rice cooker; whisk well until fairly smooth.*
2. *Close lid and press COOK.*
3. *When rice cooker switches to WARM (about 6-7 minutes), wait for 5-6 minutes then press COOK again; repeat if necessary.*
4. *Cooking is complete after about 20 minutes of cooking or when a wooden pick inserted slightly off-center comes out with just a few moist crumbs clinging to it.*
5. *Spoon into serving dishes, garnish as desired and serve.*

TIP
For a decadent version, double up on the chocolate chips and mix them up using white or butterscotch chips.

CHEESY PEPPERONI
DINNER

	1.5 CUP (3 CUPS COOKED) 1-2 SERVINGS	3 CUP (6 CUPS COOKED) 3-4 SERVINGS	5 CUP (10 CUPS COOKED) 5-6 SERVINGS
SMALL SHELL SHAPED PASTA, UNCOOKED	1/2 CUP	1 CUP	1 1/2 CUPS
PASTA SAUCE, JARRED	1/2 CUP	1 CUP	1 1/2 CUPS
KOSHER SALT AND FRESHLY GROUND PEPPER	TO TASTE	TO TASTE	TO TASTE
PEPPERONI SLICES, JULIENNED	1/3 CUP	2/3 CUP	1 CUP
WHITE WINE OR WATER	1/4 CUP	1/2 CUP	3/4 CUP
FRESH KALE, JULIENNED	1/2 CUP	1 CUP	1 1/2 CUPS
PARMESAN CHEESE, GRATED	1/4 CUP	1/2 CUP	3/4 CUP
FRESH MOZZARELLA, DICED	1/4 CUP	1/2 CUP	3/4 CUP

Method:

1. *Combine all ingredients, except mozzarella, in the rice cooker and stir.*
2. *Close lid and press COOK.*
3. *Cook for 20-25 minutes or until pasta is tender, stirring occasionally.*
4. *Spoon into a serving dish.*
5. *Top with mozzarella, garnish as desired and serve.*

CHERRY
COBBLER

	1.5 CUP (3 CUPS COOKED) 1-2 SERVINGS	3 CUP (6 CUPS COOKED) 3-4 SERVINGS	5 CUP (10 CUPS COOKED) 5-6 SERVINGS
FROZEN CHERRIES, THAWED	1 1/2 CUPS	3 CUPS	4 1/2 CUPS
GRANULATED SUGAR	1/3 CUP	2/3 CUP	1 CUP
UNSALTED BUTTER	1 TBSP	2 TBSP	3 TBSP
KOSHER SALT	1/4 tsp	1/2 tsp	3/4 tsp
LEMON JUICE	1 tsp	2 tsp	3 tsp
CORNSTARCH	1 TBSP	2 TBSP	3 TBSP
GRANOLA, STORE-BOUGHT	1/2 CUP	1 CUP	1 1/2 CUPS
VANILLA ICE CREAM FOR SERVING	AS DESIRED	AS DESIRED	AS DESIRED

Method:

1. *Combine all ingredients, except granola and ice cream, in the rice cooker.*
2. *Stir well, close lid and press COOK.*
3. *Cook for 20-25 minutes or until thick and bubbly, stirring occasionally.*
4. *When cooking is complete, spoon into serving dishes and top with granola and ice cream.*
5. *Garnish as desired and serve.*

TIP
This cobbler is great with any type of frozen berries or fruit such as peaches.

EASY CRUST
BACON QUICHE

	1.5 CUP (3 CUPS COOKED) 1-2 SERVINGS	3 CUP (6 CUPS COOKED) 3-4 SERVINGS	5 CUP (10 CUPS COOKED) 5-6 SERVINGS
BUTTER, UNSALTED	1 TBSP	2 TBSP	3 TBSP
WHITE BREAD SLICES	1	2	3
BACON STRIPS, COOKED AND CRUMBLED	3	6	9
LARGE EGGS	3	6	9
GREEN ONIONS, SLICED	1	2	3
PARMESAN CHEESE, GRATED	1/4 CUP	1/2 CUP	3/4 CUP
HEAVY CREAM OR HALF & HALF	2 TBSP	1/4 CUP	1/3 CUP
KOSHER SALT AND FRESHLY GROUND PEPPER	TO TASTE	TO TASTE	TO TASTE

Method:

1. Butter one side of the bread and press it butter-side down into the bottom of the rice cooker.
2. In a small bowl, whisk together remaining ingredients until blended.
3. Pour mixture over the bread, close lid and press COOK.
4. When rice cooker switches to KEEP WARM (about 6-7 minutes), wait for 5-6 minutes then press COOK again; repeat if necessary.
5. Cooking is complete after 20-25 minutes or when quiche is just set.
6. Using a silicone spatula, gently tip quiche out onto a plate.
7. Garnish as desired and serve.

RICE COOKER RECIPES

CURRY
CHICKEN

	1.5 CUP (3 CUPS COOKED) 1-2 SERVINGS	3 CUP (6 CUPS COOKED) 3-4 SERVINGS	5 CUP (10 CUPS COOKED) 5-6 SERVINGS
CHICKEN TENDERS, RAW, DICED	3	6	9
KOSHER SALT	TO TASTE	TO TASTE	TO TASTE
COCONUT OIL	1 TBSP	2 TBSP	3 TBSP
YELLOW ONIONS, CHOPPED	2 TBSP	1/4 CUP	1/3 CUP
GARLIC CLOVE, CHOPPED	1 TBSP	2 TBSP	3 TBSP
GINGER, CHOPPED	1 TBSP	2 TBSP	3 TBSP
CURRY POWDER	1 TBSP	2 TBSP	3 TBSP
HOT PEPPER SAUCE, BOTTLED (OPTIONAL)	1/8 tsp	1/4 tsp	1/2 tsp
COCONUT MILK	1/2 CUP	1 CUP	1 1/2 CUPS
ALL PURPOSE FLOUR	1 TBSP	2 TBSP	3 TBSP
PERFECT WHITE RICE (SEE PAGE 11) FOR SERVING	AS DESIRED	AS DESIRED	AS DESIRED

Method:

1. *Place the chicken, salt, coconut oil, onions, garlic, ginger, curry powder and hot sauce in the rice cooker; stir well.*
2. *In a small bowl, whisk together the coconut milk and flour then pour over the chicken mixture.*
3. *Close lid and press COOK.*
4. *Cook for 20-25 minutes or until chicken is cooked through and sauce is thick and bubbly.*
5. *When cooking is complete, garnish as desired and serve with Perfect White Rice.*

DAD'S TURN TO COOK
PASTA

	1.5 CUP (3 CUPS COOKED) 1-2 SERVINGS	3 CUP (6 CUPS COOKED) 3-4 SERVINGS	5 CUP (10 CUPS COOKED) 5-6 SERVINGS
PORK SAUSAGE, COOKED	1/2 CUP	1 CUP	1 1/2 CUPS
SMALL SIZE PASTA, DRY	1/2 CUP	1 CUP	1 1/2 CUPS
PASTA SAUCE, JARRED	1/2 CUP	1 CUP	1 1/2 CUPS
WATER OR CHICKEN STOCK	1/4 CUP	1/2 CUP	3/4 CUP
RICOTTA CHEESE	2 TBSP	1/4 CUP	1/3 CUP
ITALIAN DRESSING, BOTTLED	2 TBSP	1/4 CUP	1/3 CUP
KOSHER SALT AND FRESHLY GROUND PEPPER	TO TASTE	TO TASTE	TO TASTE
ITALIAN BLEND CHEESE, SHREDDED	1/4 CUP	1/2 CUP	3/4 CUP

Method:

1. *Combine all ingredients in the rice cooker and stir.*
2. *Close lid and press COOK.*
3. *Cook for 20-25 minutes or until pasta is tender.*
4. *When cooking is complete, garnish as desired and serve.*

TIP

As an alternative to the pork sausage, you can use the bags of ready-cooked turkey sausage crumbles available in 9.6 oz bags in the grocery store isle next to the bacon. They are a wonderful time saver.

CHICKEN & BISCUIT
BAKE

	1.5 CUP (3 CUPS COOKED) 1-2 SERVINGS	3 CUP (6 CUPS COOKED) 3-4 SERVINGS	5 CUP (10 CUPS COOKED) 5-6 SERVINGS
REFRIGERATOR-STYLE BISCUITS	5	8	12
CANNED CREAM OF CHICKEN SOUP (14 OZ SIZE)	1 CAN	2 CANS	3 CANS
WHOLE MILK	1 CUP	2 CUPS	3 CUPS
CHICKEN TENDERS, RAW, DICED	3	6	9
FROZEN MIXED VEGETABLES	1/4 CUP	1/2 CUP	3/4 CUP
FRESHLY GROUND PEPPER	TO TASTE	TO TASTE	TO TASTE

Method:

1. *Apply nonstick cooking spray to the rice cooker.*
2. *Place the biscuits in the bottom of the rice cooker.*
3. *Close lid and press COOK.*
4. *Cook for 10 minutes or until rice cooker switches to WARM.*
5. *Turn biscuits over then cook for an additional 10 minutes.*
6. *Remove biscuits and set aside.*
7. *Combine remaining ingredients in the rice cooker and stir.*
8. *Close lid and press COOK.*
9. *Cook for 20-25 minutes or until chicken is cooked through and sauce is thick and bubbly.*
10. *When cooking is complete, top with the biscuits, garnish as desired and serve.*

EASY ENCHILADA
BAKE

	1.5 CUP (3 CUPS COOKED) 1-2 SERVINGS	3 CUP (6 CUPS COOKED) 3-4 SERVINGS	5 CUP (10 CUPS COOKED) 5-6 SERVINGS
CHICKEN TENDERS, RAW	3	6	9
CANNED ENCHILADA SAUCE (13 OZ SIZE)	1 CAN	2 CANS	3 CANS
CANNED GREEN CHILIES (4 OZ SIZE)	1 CAN	2 CANS	3 CANS
TORTILLA CHIPS, CRUSHED (PLUS MORE FOR SERVING)	1 1/2 CUPS	3 CUPS	4 1/2 CUPS
MEXICAN CHEESE BLEND, SHREDDED	1/4 CUP	1/2 CUP	3/4 CUP
JALAPEÑO PEPPER, SLICED	TO TASTE	TO TASTE	TO TASTE
KOSHER SALT	TO TASTE	TO TASTE	TO TASTE

Method:

1. *Combine all ingredients in the rice cooker and stir.*
2. *Close lid and press COOK.*
3. *Cook for 20-25 minutes or until chicken is cooked through and mixture is thick and bubbly.*
4. *When cooking is complete, garnish as desired and serve.*

MARGARITA
SHRIMP

	1.5 CUP (3 CUPS COOKED) 1-2 SERVINGS	3 CUP (6 CUPS COOKED) 3-4 SERVINGS	5 CUP (10 CUPS COOKED) 5-6 SERVINGS
MARGARITA MIX, BOTTLED	1/2 CUP	1 CUP	1 1/2 CUPS
ALL PURPOSE FLOUR	1 TBSP	2 TBSP	3 TBSP
SHRIMP, UNCOOKED	8 OZ	1 POUND	1 1/2 POUNDS
OLIVE OIL	1 TBSP	2 TBSP	3 TBSP
GARLIC CLOVES, CHOPPED	2	4	6
KOSHER SALT AND FRESHLY GROUND PEPPER	TO TASTE	TO TASTE	TO TASTE
FRESH PARSLEY, CHOPPED	1 TBSP	2 TBSP	3 TBSP
SUSHI RICE FOR SERVING (SEE PAGE 90)	AS DESIRED	AS DESIRED	AS DESIRED

Method:

1. In a small bowl, whisk together the margarita mix and flour until smooth.
2. Pour mixture into the rice cooker.
3. Add remaining ingredients, except sushi rice, to the rice cooker; stir to combine.
4. Close lid and press COOK.
5. Cook for 15-20 minutes or until sauce is thick and bubbly.
6. When cooking is complete, garnish as desired and serve over rice.

RICE COOKER RECIPES

63

PORK CHOP
PASTA

	1.5 CUP (3 CUPS COOKED) 1-2 SERVINGS	3 CUP (6 CUPS COOKED) 3-4 SERVINGS	5 CUP (10 CUPS COOKED) 5-6 SERVINGS
BONELESS PORK CHOP, RAW, THINLY SLICED	1	3	5
PENNE PASTA, DRY	1/2 CUP	1 CUP	1 1/2 CUPS
YELLOW ONION, CHOPPED	2 TBSP	1/4 CUP	1/3 CUP
CHICKEN-FLAVORED BASE, STORE-BOUGHT	1 TBSP	2 TBSP	3 TBSP
WHITE WINE	1 TBSP	2 TBSP	3 TBSP
DRY THYME	1/4 tsp	1/2 tsp	3/4 tsp
WHOLE MILK	1/2 CUP	1 CUP	1 1/2 CUPS
KOSHER SALT AND FRESHLY GROUND PEPPER	TO TASTE	TO TASTE	TO TASTE
BROCCOLI FLORETS, FRESH OR FROZEN	1/2 CUP	1 CUP	1 1/2 CUPS

Method:

1. *Place the pork chop in the rice cooker.*
2. *In a mixing bowl, stir together remaining ingredients then pour into the rice cooker.*
3. *Close lid and press COOK.*
4. *Cook for 20-25 minutes or until pork is cooked through and pasta is tender.*
5. *When cooking is complete, garnish as desired and serve.*

TIP

For crisper broccoli, add it after the other ingredients have been cooking for 15 minutes.

GLAZED
CINNAMON APPLES

	1.5 CUP (3 CUPS COOKED) 1-2 SERVINGS	3 CUP (6 CUPS COOKED) 3-4 SERVINGS	5 CUP (10 CUPS COOKED) 5-6 SERVINGS
GRANNY SMITH APPLES, SLICED	1	3	6
UNSALTED BUTTER	1 TBSP	3 TBSP	5 TBSP
LIGHT BROWN SUGAR, PACKED	1 TBSP	3 TBSP	5 TBSP
ALL PURPOSE FLOUR	2 tsp	2 TBSP	3 TBSP
APPLE JUICE OR WATER	1 TBSP	1/4 CUP	1/2 CUP
GROUND CINNAMON	1/2 tsp	1 tsp	1 1/2 tsp
KOSHER SALT	TO TASTE	TO TASTE	TO TASTE

Method:

1. Combine all ingredients in the rice cooker and stir well.
2. Close lid and press COOK.
3. Cook for 25-30 minutes or until apples are soft and sauce is thick and bubbly.
4. When cooking is complete, garnish as desired and serve.

GARLIC MASHED
POTATOES

	1.5 CUP (3 CUPS COOKED) 1-2 SERVINGS	3 CUP (6 CUPS COOKED) 3-4 SERVINGS	5 CUP (10 CUPS COOKED) 5-6 SERVINGS
RUSSET POTATO, LARGE	1	3	5
WHOLE GARLIC CLOVES	2	4	6
KOSHER SALT	TO TASTE	TO TASTE	TO TASTE
UNSALTED BUTTER	1 TBSP	3 TBSP	5 TBSP
WHOLE MILK	AS NEEDED	AS NEEDED	AS NEEDED

Method:

1. *Peel and cut potato into 1-inch cubes.*
2. *Transfer potato cubes to the rice cooker then add water to just cover the potatoes.*
3. *Add the garlic and salt to the rice cooker.*
4. *Close lid and press COOK.*
5. *Cook for 20-25 minutes or until potatoes are fork tender.*
6. *When cooking is complete, carefully drain off all the water.*
7. *Mash the potatoes while adding the butter until mostly smooth.*
8. *Stir in some milk until potatoes are creamy to your liking.*
9. *Garnish as desired and serve.*

CREAMY LINGUINI
WITH HAM

	1.5 CUP (3 CUPS COOKED) 1-2 SERVINGS	3 CUP (6 CUPS COOKED) 3-4 SERVINGS	5 CUP (10 CUPS COOKED) 5-6 SERVINGS
SMOKED HAM, DICED	1/4 CUP	1/2 CUP	3/4 CUP
LINGUINI NOODLES, BROKEN, UNCOOKED	1/2 CUP	1 CUP	1 1/2 CUPS
HALF & HALF	1/2 CUP	1 CUP	1 1/2 CUPS
YELLOW ONION, CHOPPED	2 TBSP	1/4 CUP	1/3 CUP
PARMESAN CHEESE, GRATED	1/4 CUP	1/2 CUP	3/4 CUP
CHICKEN-FLAVORED BASE, STORE-BOUGHT	1 tsp	2 tsp	1 TBSP
KOSHER SALT AND FRESHLY GROUND PEPPER	TO TASTE	TO TASTE	TO TASTE
FROZEN PEAS	1/4 CUP	1/2 CUP	3/4 CUP

Method:

1. *Combine all ingredients in the rice cooker and stir.*
2. *Close lid and press COOK.*
3. *Cook for 20-25 minutes or until noodles are tender, stirring occasionally.*
4. *Pour into a serving dish, garnish as desired and serve.*

HERBED CHEESY
BISCUITS

	1.5 CUP (3 CUPS COOKED) 1-2 SERVINGS	3 CUP (6 CUPS COOKED) 3-4 SERVINGS	5 CUP (10 CUPS COOKED) 5-6 SERVINGS
UNSALTED BUTTER, MELTED	1 TBSP	2 TBSP	3 TBSP
WHOLE GARLIC CLOVE, CHOPPED	1	2	3
SPRIG OF THYME, CHOPPED	1	2	3
CHEDDAR CHEESE, SHREDDED	1/4 CUP	1/2 CUP	3/4 CUP
REFRIGERATOR-STYLE BISCUITS	5	8	10

Method:

1. *Combine all ingredients, except biscuits, in the rice cooker and stir.*
2. *Place the biscuits in a single layer over the rice cooker contents then gently press down.*
3. *Close lid and press COOK.*
4. *When rice cooker switches to KEEP WARM (about 6-7 minutes), wait for 5-6 minutes then press COOK again; repeat if necessary.*
5. *Cooking is complete after about 20-25 minutes or when biscuits are dull and pale in color and a wooden pick inserted into a biscuit comes out clean.*
6. *Invert onto a plate so that the brown bottom is on top.*
7. *Garnish as desired and serve.*

HONEY GLAZED
CARROTS

	1.5 CUP (3 CUPS COOKED) 1-2 SERVINGS	3 CUP (6 CUPS COOKED) 3-4 SERVINGS	5 CUP (10 CUPS COOKED) 5-6 SERVINGS
MEDIUM CARROTS, PEELED AND SLICED	3	6	9
UNSALTED BUTTER	2 TBSP	1/4 CUP	1/3 CUP
APPLE CIDER VINEGAR	1 tsp	2 tsp	1 TBSP
HONEY	3 TBSP	1/3 CUP	1/2 CUP
ALL PURPOSE FLOUR	2 tsp	1 TBSP+1 tsp	2 TBSP
KOSHER SALT AND FRESHLY GROUND PEPPER	TO TASTE	TO TASTE	TO TASTE
FRESH PARSLEY FOR SERVING	AS DESIRED	AS DESIRED	AS DESIRED

Method:

1. Combine all ingredients, except parsley, in the rice cooker.
2. Stir well until flour is lump-free then close lid and press COOK.
3. Cook for 18-20 minutes or until carrots are tender and glaze is thick and bubbly.
4. When cooking is complete, sprinkle with parsley, garnish as desired and serve.

TIP

For a delicious vegan version, substitute an equal amount of coconut oil for the butter in this recipe.

SHRIMP & SAUSAGE
JAMBALAYA

	1.5 CUP (3 CUPS COOKED) 1-2 SERVINGS	3 CUP (6 CUPS COOKED) 3-4 SERVINGS	5 CUP (10 CUPS COOKED) 5-6 SERVINGS
KIELBASA, COOKED	1/4 CUP	1/2 CUP	3/4 CUP
SHRIMP, UNCOOKED	6	12	18
BASMATI WHITE RICE, UNCOOKED	1/2 CUP	1 CUP	1 1/2 CUPS
OLIVE OIL	1 TBSP	2 TBSP	3 TBSP
YELLOW ONIONS, DICED	1/4 CUP	1/2 CUP	3/4 CUP
BELL PEPPERS, DICED	1/4 CUP	1/2 CUP	3/4 CUP
CELERY, DICED	1/4 CUP	1/2 CUP	3/4 CUP
GARLIC CLOVES, CHOPPED	1	2	3
SMALL TOMATO, CHOPPED	1	2	3
CHICKEN STOCK	1/2 CUP	1 CUP	1 1/2 CUPS
KOSHER SALT AND FRESHLY GROUND PEPPER	TO TASTE	TO TASTE	TO TASTE
SMALL BAY LEAF	1	2	3
CHILI FLAKES (OPTIONAL)	AS DESIRED	AS DESIRED	AS DESIRED

Method:

1. *Combine all ingredients in the rice cooker and stir well.*
2. *Close lid and press COOK.*
3. *Cook for 25-30 minutes or until rice cooker switches to WARM.*
4. *When cooking is complete, garnish as desired and serve.*

TIP

If you're in a hurry, you can substitute a frozen bag of diced peppers, onions and garlic (available in the frozen food section of your grocery store) for the fresh veggies in this recipe. You might need to adjust your cooking time by a few minutes if needed.

KICKED UP
RAMEN

	1.5 CUP (3 CUPS COOKED) 1-2 SERVINGS	3 CUP (6 CUPS COOKED) 3-4 SERVINGS	5 CUP (10 CUPS COOKED) 5-6 SERVINGS
RAMEN NOODLES (3 OZ PACKAGE), BROKEN UP, UNCOOKED	1	2	3
WATER	1 1/4 CUPS	2 1/2 CUPS	3 3/4 CUPS
LEFTOVER CHICKEN, COOKED	1/2 CUP	1 CUP	1 1/2 CUPS
SNOW PEAS, FRESH	1/4 CUP	1/2 CUP	3/4 CUP
SMALL CARROTS, SLICED	1	2	3
DARK SESAME OIL	1 tsp	2 tsp	1 TBSP
GARLIC CLOVES, CHOPPED	1	2	3
FRESH GINGER, CHOPPED	1 tsp	2 tsp	1 TBSP
SOY SAUCE	TO TASTE	TO TASTE	TO TASTE
SRIRACHA HOT SAUCE, BOTTLED (OPTIONAL)	AS DESIRED	AS DESIRED	AS DESIRED

Method:

1. *Combine all ingredients, including the ramen seasoning packet contents, in the rice cooker.*
2. *Stir well then close lid and press COOK.*
3. *Set a kitchen timer for 10 minutes.*
4. *Cooking is complete when timer rings or when noodles and vegetables are tender.*
5. *Garnish as desired before serving.*

MEATBALLS
IN SAUCE

	1.5 CUP (3 CUPS COOKED) 1-2 SERVINGS	3 CUP (6 CUPS COOKED) 3-4 SERVINGS	5 CUP (10 CUPS COOKED) 5-6 SERVINGS
FROZEN MEATBALLS	8	16	24
PASTA SAUCE, JARRED	1 1/2 CUPS	3 CUPS	4 1/2 CUPS
WHITE WINE	1/4 CUP	1/2 CUP	3/4 CUP
ITALIAN DRESSING, STORE-BOUGHT	1 TBSP	2 TBSP	3 TBSP
PARMESAN CHEESE, GRATED + MORE FOR SERVING	2 TBSP	1/4 CUP	1/3 CUP
KOSHER SALT AND FRESHLY GROUND PEPPER	TO TASTE	TO TASTE	TO TASTE

Method:

1. *Combine all ingredients in the rice cooker and stir.*
2. *Close lid and press COOK.*
3. *Cook for 20-25 minutes or until meatballs are hot and sauce is bubbly.*
4. *When cooking is complete, top with additional cheese, garnish as desired and serve.*

TIP

These are great served with the Easiest Buttered Noodles on page 26.

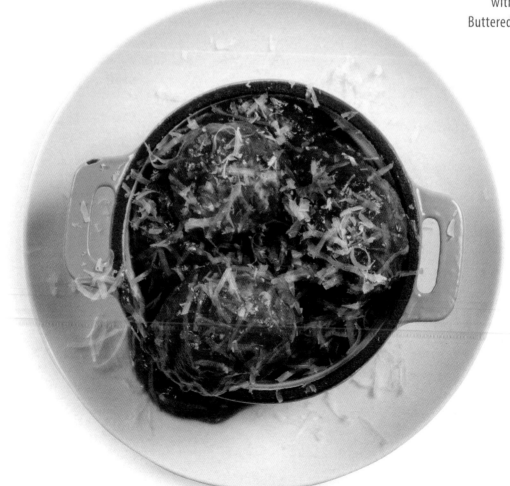

MEATLESS
MONDAY RICE

	1.5 CUP (3 CUPS COOKED) 1-2 SERVINGS	3 CUP (6 CUPS COOKED) 3-4 SERVINGS	5 CUP (10 CUPS COOKED) 5-6 SERVINGS
UNSALTED BUTTER	2 TBSP	1/4 CUP	1/3 CUP
GARLIC CLOVES, CHOPPED	3	6	9
YELLOW ONIONS, SLICED	1/4 CUP	1/2 CUP	3/4 CUP
BASMATI WHITE RICE, UNCOOKED	1/2 CUP	1 CUP	1 1/2 CUPS
VEGETABLE STOCK	1/2 CUP	1 CUP	1 1/2 CUPS
PARMESAN CHEESE, GRATED	2 TBSP	1/4 CUP	1/3 CUP
KOSHER SALT AND FRESHLY GROUND PEPPER	TO TASTE	TO TASTE	TO TASTE
MUSHROOMS, SLICED	1/4 CUP	1/2 CUP	3/4 CUP
FROZEN MIXED VEGETABLES	1/4 CUP	1/2 CUP	3/4 CUP
SMALL TOMATOES, DICED	1	2	3

Method:

1. *Combine all ingredients in the rice cooker and stir.*
2. *Close lid and press COOK.*
3. *Cook for 25-30 minutes or until rice cooker switches to WARM.*
4. *When cooking is complete, garnish as desired and serve.*

PORK CHOP &
STUFFING BAKE

	1.5 CUP (3 CUPS COOKED) 1-2 SERVINGS	3 CUP (6 CUPS COOKED) 3-4 SERVINGS	5 CUP (10 CUPS COOKED) 5-6 SERVINGS
BONELESS PORK CHOPS, RAW, THIN CUT	1	3	5
STOVE TOP STYLE STUFFING MIX	1 CUP	2 CUPS	3 CUPS
UNSALTED BUTTER, MELTED	1 TBSP	2 TBSP	3 TBSP
YELLOW ONIONS, CHOPPED	2 TBSP	1/4 CUP	1/3 CUP
SMALL CELERY STALK, CHOPPED	1	2	3
WATER	1 1/2 CUPS	3 CUPS	4 1/2 CUPS
KOSHER SALT AND FRESHLY GROUND PEPPER	TO TASTE	TO TASTE	TO TASTE

Method:

1. *Place the pork chop in the rice cooker.*
2. *In a bowl, combine remaining ingredients then pour over pork chop in the rice cooker.*
3. *Close lid and press COOK.*
4. *Cook for 35-40 minutes or until pork chop is fork tender.*
5. *When cooking is complete, garnish as desired and serve.*

OLD FASHIONED
BEEF STEW

	1.5 CUP (3 CUPS COOKED) 1-2 SERVINGS	3 CUP (6 CUPS COOKED) 3-4 SERVINGS	5 CUP (10 CUPS COOKED) 5-6 SERVINGS
BEEF STEW MEAT, RAW, DICED SMALL	8 OZ	1 POUND	1 1/2 POUNDS
SMALL RED BLISS POTATOES, DICED	2	4	6
SMALL CARROT, DICED	1	2	3
SMALL YELLOW ONION, DICED	1	2	3
BEEF STOCK	1/2 CUP	1 CUP	1 1/2 CUPS
KETCHUP	1 TBSP	2 TBSP	3 TBSP
BAY LEAF	1	2	3
ALL PURPOSE FLOUR	1 TBSP	2 TBSP	3 TBSP
KOSHER SALT AND FRESHLY GROUND PEPPER	TO TASTE	TO TASTE	TO TASTE

Method:

1. Combine all ingredients in the rice cooker; stir well until flour is lump-free.
2. Close lid and press COOK.
3. Cook for 40-45 minutes or until beef is tender and sauce is thick and bubbly.
4. When cooking is complete, garnish as desired and serve.

RICE COOKER RECIPES

QUINOA
MEDLEY

	1.5 CUP (3 CUPS COOKED) 1-2 SERVINGS	3 CUP (6 CUPS COOKED) 3-4 SERVINGS	5 CUP (10 CUPS COOKED) 5-6 SERVINGS
RED QUINOA, UNCOOKED	1 CUP	2 CUPS	3 CUPS
APPLE JUICE	1 CUP	2 CUPS	3 CUPS
VEGETABLE-FLAVORED BASE, STORE-BOUGHT	1 TBSP	2 TBSP	3 TBSP
GROUND SAGE	1/4 tsp	1/2 tsp	3/4 tsp
APPLE CIDER VINEGAR	1 tsp	2 tsp	1 TBSP
KOSHER SALT AND FRESHLY GROUND PEPPER	TO TASTE	TO TASTE	TO TASTE
GARLIC CLOVES, CHOPPED	2	4	6
SMALL APPLE, CHOPPED	1	2	3
SMALL CELERY STALK, CHOPPED	1	2	3
RAISINS	2 TBSP	1/4 CUP	1/3 CUP
FRESH SPINACH LEAVES	1 CUP	2 CUPS	3 CUPS

Method:

1. Combine all ingredients in the rice cooker.
2. Stir well then close lid and press COOK.
3. Cook for 20-25 minutes or until rice cooker switches to WARM.
4. When cooking is complete, garnish as desired and serve.

TIP

For brighter colored spinach, add it 15 minutes into the cooking.

VEGGIES YOUR KIDS
WILL EAT

	1.5 CUP (3 CUPS COOKED) 1-2 SERVINGS	3 CUP (6 CUPS COOKED) 3-4 SERVINGS	5 CUP (10 CUPS COOKED) 5-6 SERVINGS
UNSALTED BUTTER	1 TBSP	2 TBSP	3 TBSP
VEGETABLE STOCK	2 TBSP	1/4 CUP	1/3 CUP
HONEY	2 tsp	1 TBSP+1 tsp	2 TBSP
KOSHER SALT	TO TASTE	TO TASTE	TO TASTE
SMALL CARROT, SLICED	1	2	3
FRESH GREEN BEANS, SLICED	1 CUP	2 CUPS	3 CUPS
FRESH CORN KERNELS	1/4 CUP	1/2 CUP	3/4 CUP

Method:

1. *Combine all ingredients in the rice cooker and stir.*
2. *Close lid and press COOK.*
3. *Cook for 10-15 minutes or until vegetables are just tender.*
4. *When cooking is complete, serve as desired.*

TIP
Try letting your picky children eat with chopsticks. My boys would eat almost anything when they were little if I gave them chopsticks.

CHOCOLATE
FONDUE

	1.5 CUP (3 CUPS COOKED) 1-2 SERVINGS	3 CUP (6 CUPS COOKED) 3-4 SERVINGS	5 CUP (10 CUPS COOKED) 5-6 SERVINGS
UNSALTED BUTTER	1 TBSP	2 TBSP	3 TBSP
HEAVY CREAM	1/2 CUP	1 CUP	1 1/2 CUPS
SEMI-SWEET CHOCOLATE CHIPS	1/2 CUP	1 CUP	1 1/2 CUPS
VANILLA EXTRACT	1 tsp	2 tsp	1 TBSP
ASSORTED FRUITS AND COOKIES FOR SERVING	AS DESIRED	AS DESIRED	AS DESIRED

Method:

1. Combine the butter and cream in the rice cooker.
2. Do not cover and press COOK.
3. After 6-8 minutes or when mixture simmers, switch rice cooker to WARM.
4. Pour the chocolate and vanilla into the rice cooker and let stand for 30 seconds to soften.
5. Stir mixture using a spatula until smooth, shiny and chocolate is melted.
6. Serve with assorted fruits and cookies as dippers.

TIP

You can turn this into white chocolate fondue by substituting white chocolate chips for the semi-sweet but you need to increase the amount to 1 cup.

VEGETARIAN PASTA &
SWEET POTATO

	1.5 CUP (3 CUPS COOKED) 1-2 SERVINGS	3 CUP (6 CUPS COOKED) 3-4 SERVINGS	5 CUP (10 CUPS COOKED) 5-6 SERVINGS
YELLOW ONIONS, SLICED	1/4 CUP	1/2 CUP	1 1/2 CUPS
SWEET POTATO, DICED	1/2 CUP	1 CUP	1 1/2 CUPS
BOW TIE PASTA, UNCOOKED	1/2 CUP	1 CUP	1 1/2 CUPS
VEGETABLE STOCK	1/2 CUP	1 CUP	1 1/2 CUPS
KOSHER SALT AND FRESHLY GROUND PEPPER	TO TASTE	TO TASTE	TO TASTE
BALSAMIC VINEGAR	2 tsp	1 TBSP+1 tsp	2 TBSP
FRESH SPINACH LEAVES	1 CUP	2 CUPS	3 CUPS
PARMESAN CHEESE, GRATED	2 TBSP	1/4 CUP	1/3 CUP

Method:

1. Combine all ingredients, except spinach and cheese, in the rice cooker and stir.
2. Close lid and press COOK.
3. Cook for 20-25 minutes or until pasta is tender.
4. Add spinach and cheese (rice cooker will be very full) then stir gently for 1 minute or until spinach just begins to wilt.
5. Remove, garnish as desired and serve.

PASTA
PRIMAVERA

	1.5 CUP (3 CUPS COOKED) 1-2 SERVINGS	3 CUP (6 CUPS COOKED) 3-4 SERVINGS	5 CUP (10 CUPS COOKED) 5-6 SERVINGS
OLIVE OIL	1 TBSP	2 TBSP	3 TBSP
BELL PEPPERS, SLICED	1/4 CUP	1/2 CUP	3/4 CUP
SMALL CARROT, SLICED	1	2	3
SMALL ZUCCHINI, SLICED	1	2	3
GARLIC CLOVES, CHOPPED	2	4	6
BOW TIE PASTA, UNCOOKED	1/2 CUP	1 CUP	1 1/2 CUPS
VEGETABLE STOCK	1/2 CUP	1 CUP	1 1/2 CUPS
KOSHER SALT AND FRESHLY GROUND PEPPER	TO TASTE	TO TASTE	TO TASTE
PARMESAN CHEESE, GRATED	1/4 CUP	1/2 CUP	3/4 CUP
FRESH BASIL LEAVES FOR SERVING	AS DESIRED	AS DESIRED	AS DESIRED

Method:

1. Combine all ingredients, except basil, in the rice cooker.
2. Stir well, close lid and press COOK.
3. Cook for 20-25 minutes or until pasta is tender.
4. When cooking is complete, top with fresh basil, garnish as desired and serve.

POACHED
EGGS

	1.5 CUP (3 CUPS COOKED) 1-2 SERVINGS	3 CUP (6 CUPS COOKED) 3-4 SERVINGS	5 CUP (10 CUPS COOKED) 5-6 SERVINGS
WATER	1 CUP	2 CUPS	3 CUPS
KOSHER SALT	TO TASTE	TO TASTE	TO TASTE
LARGE EGGS (AS FRESH AS POSSIBLE)	1	2	3

Method:

1. *Place water and some salt in the rice cooker.*
2. *Close lid and press COOK.*
3. *Set a kitchen timer for 10 minutes.*
4. *After 10 minutes, the water in rice cooker should be boiling.*
5. *Crack egg into a small bowl then switch rice cooker to WARM.*
6. *Tip egg into a small, fine meshed strainer and let the watery part of the egg white flow out; discard this part.*
7. *Lower the strainer with remaining egg into the simmering water inside the rice cooker; tip from side to side to loosen the egg from the strainer then tip egg out of the strainer into the water using a spatula if necessary.*
8. *Set a kitchen timer for exactly 4 minutes for soft yolk, 5 minutes for medium and 6 minutes for hard yolk.*
9. *When timer rings, gently remove the egg using a slotted spoon.*
10. *Drain on a paper towel and serve as desired.*

RICE
PUDDING

	1.5 CUP (3 CUPS COOKED) 1-2 SERVINGS	3 CUP (6 CUPS COOKED) 3-4 SERVINGS	5 CUP (10 CUPS COOKED) 5-6 SERVINGS
WHOLE MILK OR ALMOND MILK	1 1/4 CUPS	2 1/2 CUPS	3 3/4 CUPS
SHORT-GRAIN WHITE RICE, UNCOOKED	3 TBSP	1/4 CUP + 2 TBSP	1/2 CUP +1 TBSP
GRANULATED SUGAR	2 TBSP	1/4 CUP	1/3 CUP
VANILLA EXTRACT	1/4 tsp	1/2 tsp	3/4 tsp
KOSHER SALT	A PINCH	2 PINCHES	3 PINCHES

Method:

1. *Combine all ingredients in the rice cooker and stir well.*
2. *Close lid and press COOK.*
3. *Cook for 30-35 minutes or until rice is tender and mixture is thick and bubbly.*
4. *When cooking is complete, garnish as desired and serve.*

TIP

Do not attempt to double the recipe
as the milk tends to boil over.

WOLF'S FAMOUS
REISFLEISCH

	1.5 CUP (3 CUPS COOKED) 1-2 SERVINGS	3 CUP (6 CUPS COOKED) 3-4 SERVINGS	5 CUP (10 CUPS COOKED) 5-6 SERVINGS
BASMATI WHITE RICE, UNCOOKED	1/3 CUP	2/3 CUP	1 CUP
PAPRIKA	1 tsp	2 tsp	1 TBSP
CHILI FLAKES (OPTIONAL)	AS DESIRED	AS DESIRED	AS DESIRED
CELERY, DICED	2 TBSP	1/4 CUP	1/3 CUP
YELLOW ONIONS, DICED	2 TBSP	1/4 CUP	1/3 CUP
BELL PEPPERS	2 TBSP	1/4 CUP	1/3 CUP
WHOLE GARLIC CLOVES, CHOPPED	1	2	3
KIELBASA SAUSAGE, DICED	1/3 CUP	2/3 CUP	1 CUP
UNSALTED BUTTER	1 TBSP	2 TBSP	3 TBSP
KOSHER SALT AND FRESHLY GROUND PEPPER	TO TASTE	TO TASTE	TO TASTE
WATER	1/3 CUP	2/3 CUP	1 CUP
CHICKEN-FLAVORED BASE, STORE-BOUGHT	2 tsp	1 TBSP+1 tsp	2 TBSP

Method:

1. *Combine all ingredients in the rice cooker and stir.*
2. *Close lid and press COOK.*
3. *Cook for 20-25 minutes or until rice cooker switches to WARM.*
4. *When cooking is complete, let rice rest on WARM for 10 minutes.*
5. *Garnish as desired and serve.*

TIP

If you want to use brown basmati rice instead, simply add 2 more tablespoons of water and increase cooking time to about 40 minutes.

SMOTHERED
PORK CHOP

	1.5 CUP (3 CUPS COOKED) 1-2 SERVINGS	3 CUP (6 CUPS COOKED) 3-4 SERVINGS	5 CUP (10 CUPS COOKED) 5-6 SERVINGS
BEEF STOCK	1/2 CUP	1 CUP	1 1/2 CUPS
ALL PURPOSE FLOUR	2 tsp	1 TBSP+1 tsp	2 TBSP
BONELESS PORK CHOP, RAW, THINLY CUT	2	4	6
MUSHROOMS, SLICED	1/4 CUP	1/2 CUP	3/4 CUP
SMALL YELLOW ONION, SLICED	1	2	3
GROUND THYME	1/4 tsp	1/2 tsp	3/4 tsp
UNSALTED BUTTER	1 TBSP	2 TBSP	3 TBSP
KOSHER SALT AND FRESHLY GROUND PEPPER	TO TASTE	TO TASTE	TO TASTE

Method:

1. In a small mixing bowl, whisk together the stock and flour until smooth.
2. Pour stock mixture and remaining ingredients into the rice cooker.
3. Close lid and press COOK.
4. Cook for 25-30 minutes or until pork is fork tender and gravy is thick and bubbly.
5. When cooking is complete, garnish as desired and serve.

TUNA
RICE ROYAL

	1.5 CUP (3 CUPS COOKED) 1-2 SERVINGS	3 CUP (6 CUPS COOKED) 3-4 SERVINGS	5 CUP (10 CUPS COOKED) 5-6 SERVINGS
LEFTOVER WHITE BASMATI RICE	1/2 CUP	1 CUP	1 1/2 CUPS
CANNED TUNA, UNDRAINED (5 OZ SIZE)	1 CAN	2 CANS	3 CANS
SMALL CELERY STALK, DICED	1	2	3
YELLOW ONION, CHOPPED	2 TBSP	1/4 CUP	1/3 CUP
CANNED CREAM OF CELERY SOUP (11 OZ SIZE)	1 CAN	2 CANS	3 CANS
WHOLE MILK	1/4 CUP	1/2 CUP	3/4 CUP
SHARP CHEDDAR CHEESE, SHREDDED	2 TBSP	1/4 CUP	1/3 CUP
CANNED CHOW MEIN NOODLES, CRISPY	1/2 CUP	1 CUP	1 1/2 CUPS

Method:

1. *Combine all ingredients, except noodles, in the rice cooker and stir well.*
2. *Close lid and press COOK.*
3. *Cook for 20-25 minutes or until thick and bubbly.*
4. *When cooking is complete, top with chow mein noodles, garnish as desired and serve.*

TERIYAKI CHICKEN
TENDERS

	1.5 CUP (3 CUPS COOKED) 1-2 SERVINGS	3 CUP (6 CUPS COOKED) 3-4 SERVINGS	5 CUP (10 CUPS COOKED) 5-6 SERVINGS
CHICKEN TENDERS, RAW	3	6	9
VEGETABLE OIL	1 TBSP	2 TBSP	3 TBSP
WATER	1 TBSP	2 TBSP	3 TBSP
SMALL YELLOW ONION, SLICED	1	2	3
GARLIC CLOVES, CHOPPED	1 tsp	2 tsp	1 TBSP
FRESH GINGER, CHOPPED	1 tsp	2 tsp	1 TBSP
TERIYAKI SAUCE, BOTTLED	1/2 CUP	1 CUP	1 1/2 CUPS
GREEN ONIONS, SLICED	1	2	3
SESAME SEEDS	1 tsp	2 tsp	1 TBSP

Method:

1. *Combine all ingredients, except green onions and sesame seeds, in the rice cooker.*
2. *Stir well, close lid and press COOK.*
3. *Cook for 20-25 minutes or until chicken is cooked through and sauce is thick and bubbly.*
4. *When cooking is complete, top with green onions, sesame seeds and desired garnish before serving.*

TIP
Serve with the Sushi
Rice on page 90.

SPAGHETTI PIE

	1.5 CUP (3 CUPS COOKED) 1-2 SERVINGS	3 CUP (6 CUPS COOKED) 3-4 SERVINGS	5 CUP (10 CUPS COOKED) 5-6 SERVINGS
SPAGHETTI NOODLES, BROKEN, UNCOOKED	1/2 CUP	1 CUP	1 1/2 CUPS
PASTA SAUCE, JARRED	1/2 CUP	1 CUP	1 1/2 CUPS
CHICKEN STOCK	1/4 CUP	1/2 CUP	3/4 CUP
ITALIAN DRESSING, STORE-BOUGHT	1 TBSP	2 TBSP	3 TBSP
RICOTTA CHEESE	1/4 CUP	1/2 CUP	3/4 CUP
MOZZARELLA CHEESE, SHREDDED	1/4 CUP	1/2 CUP	3/4 CUP
PEPPERONI SLICES	1/4 CUP	1/2 CUP	3/4 CUP
KOSHER SALT AND FRESHLY GROUND PEPPER	TO TASTE	TO TASTE	TO TASTE
PARMESAN CHEESE, SHREDDED	1 TBSP	2 TBSP	3 TBSP

Method:

1. *Combine all ingredients in the rice cooker and stir.*
2. *Close lid and press COOK.*
3. *Cook for 20-25 minutes or until pasta is tender and sauce is very thick.*
4. *When cooking is complete, unmold onto serving plate, garnish as desired and serve.*

SAUSAGE & SAUERKRAUT

	1.5 CUP (3 CUPS COOKED) 1-2 SERVINGS	3 CUP (6 CUPS COOKED) 3-4 SERVINGS	5 CUP (10 CUPS COOKED) 5-6 SERVINGS
KIELBASA SAUSAGE, CHUNKED	1/2 CUP	1 CUP	1 1/2 CUPS
SAUERKRAUT, DRAINED	1 CUP	2 CUPS	3 CUPS
BEER OR WATER	1 CUP	2 CUPS	3 CUPS
SMALL CARROT, CHUNKED	1	2	3
SMALL RED BLISS POTATO, CHUNKED	2	4	6
FRESH PARSLEY, CHOPPED	1 TBSP	2 TBSP	3 TBSP
GRAINY MUSTARD	1 TBSP	2 TBSP	3 TBSP

Method:

1. Combine all ingredients in the rice cooker.
2. Close lid and press COOK.
3. Cook for 20-25 minutes or until potatoes are fork tender.
4. When cooking is complete, garnish as desired and serve.

SHRIMP &

GRITS

	1.5 CUP (3 CUPS COOKED) 1-2 SERVINGS	3 CUP (6 CUPS COOKED) 3-4 SERVINGS	5 CUP (10 CUPS COOKED) 5-6 SERVINGS
QUICK-COOKING TYPE GRITS	1/2 CUP	1 CUP	1 1/2 CUPS
WATER	1 CUP	2 CUPS	3 CUPS
WHOLE MILK OR ALMOND MILK	1 CUP	2 CUPS	3 CUPS
KOSHER SALT AND FRESHLY GROUND PEPPER	TO TASTE	TO TASTE	TO TASTE
SHRIMP, RAW	1/2 CUP	1 CUP	1 1/2 CUPS
UNSALTED BUTTER	2 TBSP	1/4 CUP	1/3 CUP
GARLIC CLOVES, CHOPPED	1	2	3
CHOPPED GREEN ONIONS FOR SERVING	1	2	3

Method:

1. *Combine all ingredients, except green onions, in the rice cooker and stir.*
2. *Close lid and press COOK.*
3. *Cook for 15-20 minutes or until grits are thick and bubbly, stirring occasionally using a potholder.*
4. *When cooking is complete, spoon into serving bowls, top with green onions, garnish as desired and serve.*

TIP

If substituting old fashioned or coarse ground grits for quick cooking grits, cook for an additional 5-10 minutes.

SUSHI RICE

	1.5 CUP (3 CUPS COOKED) 1-2 SERVINGS	3 CUP (6 CUPS COOKED) 3-4 SERVINGS	5 CUP (10 CUPS COOKED) 5-6 SERVINGS
SUSHI RICE OR SHORT-GRAIN RICE, UNCOOKED	2 CUPS	4 CUPS	6 CUPS
WATER	2 CUPS	4 CUPS	6 CUPS
SAKE (JAPANESE WINE)	1 TBSP	2 TBSP	3 TBSP
RICE VINEGAR	1 TBSP	2 TBSP	3 TBSP
GRANULATED SUGAR	1 TBSP	2 TBSP	3 TBSP
KOSHER SALT	1 tsp	2 tsp	1 TBSP

Method:

1. Place rice in a strainer and wash under cold running water for 2-3 minutes while rubbing rice grains between your fingers to remove the sticky surface starch.
2. Drain rice then transfer to the rice cooker.
3. Add the water, close lid and press COOK.
4. Cook until rice cooker switches to WARM (about 20-25 minutes).
5. Let rice rest on WARM in the rice cooker for 10 minutes.
6. While rice rests, stir together the sake, vinegar, sugar and salt.
7. Spread rice out evenly on a sheet pan then drizzle with sake mixture.
8. Toss rice gently using a silicone spatula then fan with a paper plate to cool it down.
9. Repeat until rice is fairly cool then serve as desired.

RICE COOKER RECIPES

SWEET & SOUR
PORK

	1.5 CUP (3 CUPS COOKED) 1-2 SERVINGS	3 CUP (6 CUPS COOKED) 3-4 SERVINGS	5 CUP (10 CUPS COOKED) 5-6 SERVINGS
BONELESS PORK CHOP, RAW, CUBED	1	2	3
KOSHER SALT	TO TASTE	TO TASTE	TO TASTE
BELL PEPPERS, CUBED	1/4 CUP	1/2 CUP	3/4 CUP
YELLOW ONIONS, CUBED	1/4 CUP	1/2 CUP	3/4 CUP
FRESH GINGER, CHOPPED	1 tsp	2 tsp	1 TBSP
GARLIC CLOVES, CHOPPED	1 tsp	2 tsp	1 TBSP
KETCHUP	2 TBSP	1/4 CUP	1/3 CUP
GRANULATED SUGAR	1 TBSP	2 TBSP	3 TBSP
PINEAPPLE CHUNKS	1/3 CUP	2/3 CUP	1 CUP
PINEAPPLE JUICE	1/3 CUP	2/3 CUP	1 CUP
CORNSTARCH	1 TBSP	2 TBSP	3 TBSP

Method:

1. *Combine all ingredients in the rice cooker and stir well.*
2. *Close lid and press COOK.*
3. *Cook for 20-25 minutes or until pork chop is fork tender and sauce is thick and bubbly.*
4. *When cooking is complete, garnish as desired and serve.*

SHRIMP
PAELLA

	1.5 CUP (3 CUPS COOKED) 1-2 SERVINGS	3 CUP (6 CUPS COOKED) 3-4 SERVINGS	5 CUP (10 CUPS COOKED) 5-6 SERVINGS
SHRIMP, RAW	1/2 CUP	1 CUP	1 1/2 CUPS
WHITE BASMATI RICE, UNCOOKED	1/2 CUP	1 CUP	1 1/2 CUPS
OLIVE OIL	1 TBSP	2 TBSP	3 TBSP
JARRED PIMENTO, SLICED	1 TBSP	2 TBSP	3 TBSP
WHITE WINE OR WATER	1 TBSP	2 TBSP	3 TBSP
CHICKEN STOCK	1/2 CUP	1 CUP	1 1/2 CUPS
KOSHER SALT	TO TASTE	TO TASTE	TO TASTE
GREEN OLIVES, SLICED	2 TBSP	1/4 CUP	1/3 CUP
SAFFRON THREADS	A PINCH	2 PINCHES	3 PINCHES

Method:

1. *Combine all ingredients in the rice cooker and stir well.*
2. *Close lid and press COOK.*
3. *Cook for 20-25 minutes or until rice cooker switches to WARM.*
4. *When cooking is complete, garnish as desired and serve.*

NACHO CHICKEN BAKE

	1.5 CUP (3 CUPS COOKED) 1-2 SERVINGS	3 CUP (6 CUPS COOKED) 3-4 SERVINGS	5 CUP (10 CUPS COOKED) 5-6 SERVINGS
CHICKEN TENDERS, RAW	3	6	9
CANNED TOMATOES WITH GREEN CHILIES (11 OZ SIZE)	1 CAN	2 CANS	3 CANS
KOSHER SALT	TO TASTE	TO TASTE	TO TASTE
JALAPEÑO PEPPERS, SLICED (OPTIONAL)	AS DESIRED	AS DESIRED	AS DESIRED
NACHO CHEESE-FLAVORED CHIPS, CRUSHED	3 CUPS	6 CUPS	9 CUPS
MONTERREY JACK CHEESE, SHREDDED	1/4 CUP	1/2 CUP	3/4 CUP

Method:

1. *Combine all ingredients in the rice cooker and stir.*
2. *Close lid and press COOK.*
3. *Cook for 20-25 minutes or until the chicken is cooked through and sauce is bubbly.*
4. *When cooking is complete, garnish as desired and serve with additional chips.*

TIP

To speed up preparation, you can use frozen chicken tenders. The are available "IQF" (Individually Quick Frozen) which makes them easy to store and use and no trimming is necessary.

BAKED POTATO
CASSEROLE

	1.5 CUP (3 CUPS COOKED) 1-2 SERVINGS	3 CUP (6 CUPS COOKED) 3-4 SERVINGS	5 CUP (10 CUPS COOKED) 5-6 SERVINGS
RUSSET POTATO, CUBED	1	2	3
WHOLE MILK	1/4 CUP	1/2 CUP	3/4 CUP
KOSHER SALT AND FRESHLY GROUND PEPPER	TO TASTE	TO TASTE	TO TASTE
SOUR CREAM	2 TBSP	1/4 CUP	1/3 CUP
CHEDDAR CHEESE, SHREDDED	1/3 CUP	2/3 CUP	1 CUP
COOKED BACON, CRUMBLED	1 SLICE	2 SLICES	3 SLICES
FRESH CHIVES, SNIPPED FOR SERVING	TO TASTE	TO TASTE	TO TASTE

Method:

1. Combine all ingredients, except chives, in the rice cooker and stir.
2. Close lid and press COOK.
3. Cook for 20-25 minutes or until potatoes are tender.
4. When cooking is complete, stir gently and top with chives.
5. Garnish as desired and serve.

ULTIMATE
MAC & CHEESE

	1.5 CUP (3 CUPS COOKED) 1-2 SERVINGS	3 CUP (6 CUPS COOKED) 3-4 SERVINGS	5 CUP (10 CUPS COOKED) 5-6 SERVINGS
COOKED BACON, CRUMBLED	2 STRIPS	4 STRIPS	6 STRIPS
GREEN ONION, SLICED	1	2	3
HALF & HALF	1/2 CUP	1 CUP	1 1/2 CUPS
WATER	3/4 CUP	1 1/2 CUPS	2 1/4 CUPS
CORKSCREW PASTA, UNCOOKED	3/4 CUP	1 1/2 CUPS	2 1/4 CUPS
KOSHER SALT	1/4 tsp	1/2 tsp	3/4 tsp
BLUE CHEESE CRUMBLES	2 TBSP	1/4 CUP	1/3 CUP
MONTERREY JACK CHEESE, SHREDDED	1/2 CUP	1 CUP	1 1/2 CUPS
CREAM CHEESE	2 TBSP	1/4 CUP	1/3 CUP

Method:

1. *Combine all ingredients, except the 3 cheeses, in the rice cooker.*
2. *Stir well then close lid and press COOK.*
3. *Cook for 20-25 minutes or until rice cooker switches to WARM.*
4. *Stir in the 3 cheeses thoroughly then close lid again and press COOK to allow the brown crust to form on the bottom.*
5. *Cooking is complete when rice cooker switches to WARM.*
6. *Remove, garnish as desired and serve.*

UPSIDE DOWN BACON
CORNBREAD

	1.5 CUP (3 CUPS COOKED) 1-2 SERVINGS	3 CUP (6 CUPS COOKED) 3-4 SERVINGS	5 CUP (10 CUPS COOKED) 5-6 SERVINGS
RAW BACON STRIPS, CUT IN HALF	3	6	9
YELLOW CORNMEAL	1/4 CUP	1/2 CUP	3/4 CUP
ALL PURPOSE FLOUR	1/4 CUP	1/2 CUP	3/4 CUP
LIGHT BROWN SUGAR, PACKED	1 TBSP	2 TBSP	3 TBSP
BAKING POWDER	3/4 tsp	1 1/4 tsp	2 tsp
KOSHER SALT	1/4 tsp	1/2 tsp	3/4 tsp
CANOLA OIL	2 TBSP	1/4 CUP	1/3 CUP
LARGE EGG	1	2	3

Method:

1. Microwave bacon for 2 minutes until halfway cooked.
2. Apply nonstick cooking spray to the rice cooker.
3. Place 3 bacon slices inside the rice cooker.
4. Add remaining 3 bacon slices and weave into a basket weave pattern inside the rice cooker.
5. In a small mixing bowl, stir together remaining ingredients.
6. Pour mixture over the rice cooker contents.
7. Close lid and press COOK.
8. When rice cooker switches to WARM (about 6-7 minutes), wait for 5-6 minutes then press COOK again.
9. Repeat this 1-2 more times or until top of cornbread is opaque with no shiny batter at the center (test for doneness by inserting a wooden pick off-center, it should come out clean).
10. When cooking is complete, invert cornbread onto a small plate and serve.

VEGAN CHOCOLATE
CAKE

	1.5 CUP (3 CUPS COOKED) 1-2 SERVINGS	3 CUP (6 CUPS COOKED) 3-4 SERVINGS	5 CUP (10 CUPS COOKED) 5-6 SERVINGS
COCONUT OIL OR CANOLA OIL	2 TBSP	1/4 CUP	1/3 CUP
GRANULATED SUGAR	1/3 CUP	2/3 CUP	1 CUP
ALMOND MILK OR SOY MILK	1/2 CUP	1 CUP	1 1/2 CUPS
APPLE CIDER VINEGAR	1 1/2 tsp	1 TBSP	1 1/2 TBSP
ALL PURPOSE FLOUR	3/4 CUP	1 1/2 CUPS	2 1/4 CUPS
COCOA POWDER	2 TBSP	1/4 CUP	1/3 CUP
VANILLA EXTRACT	1/2 tsp	1 tsp	1 1/2 tsp
KOSHER SALT	1/4 tsp	1/2 tsp	3/4 tsp
BAKING SODA	1/2 tsp	1 tsp	1 1/2 tsp
CHOCOLATE SAUCE, BOTTLED, FOR SERVING	AS DESIRED	AS DESIRED	AS DESIRED

Method:

1. *Combine all ingredients, except chocolate sauce, in the rice cooker; stir until blended.*
2. *Close lid and press COOK.*
3. *When rice cooker switches to WARM (about 6-7 minutes), wait for 5-6 minutes then press COOK again; repeat if necessary.*
4. *Cooking is complete after about 20 minutes of cooking or when a wooden pick inserted slightly off-center comes out with just a few moist crumbs clinging to it.*
5. *When cooking is complete, invert onto small serving plate.*
6. *Top with chocolate sauce, garnish as desired and serve.*

GREEN BEANS
WITH BACON

	1.5 CUP (3 CUPS COOKED) 1-2 SERVINGS	3 CUP (6 CUPS COOKED) 3-4 SERVINGS	5 CUP (10 CUPS COOKED) 5-6 SERVINGS
FRESH GREEN BEANS, SLICED	1 1/2 CUPS	3 CUPS	4 1/2 CUPS
RAW BACON STRIPS, DICED	2	4	6
CHICKEN STOCK	1 CUP	2 CUPS	3 CUPS
KOSHER SALT AND FRESHLY GROUND PEPPER	TO TASTE	TO TASTE	TO TASTE
GRANULATED SUGAR	1/4 tsp	1/2 tsp	3/4 tsp
HOT PEPPER SAUCE, BOTTLED (OPTIONAL)	A DASH	2 DASHES	3 DASHES

Method:

1. Combine all ingredients in the rice cooker and stir.
2. Close lid and press COOK.
3. Cook for 20-25 minutes or until beans are tender.
4. When cooking is complete, garnish as desired and serve.

STICKY SWEET POTATOES

	1.5 CUP (3 CUPS COOKED) 1-2 SERVINGS	3 CUP (6 CUPS COOKED) 3-4 SERVINGS	5 CUP (10 CUPS COOKED) 5-6 SERVINGS
SMALL SWEET POTATO, CUBED	1	2	3
UNSALTED BUTTER	1 TBSP	2 TBSP	3 TBSP
VANILLA EXTRACT	1/4 tsp	1/2 tsp	3/4 tsp
APPLE JUICE	1/3 CUP	2/3 CUP	1 CUP
LIGHT BROWN SUGAR, PACKED	1/4 CUP	1/2 CUP	3/4 CUP
PECAN PIECES, TOASTED	1/3 CUP	2/3 CUP	1 CUP
KOSHER SALT	A PINCH	2 PINCHES	3 PINCHES

Method:

1. *Combine all ingredients in the rice cooker and stir well.*
2. *Close lid and press COOK.*
3. *Cook for 20-25 minutes or until potatoes are tender and sauce is thick and bubbly.*
4. *When cooking is complete, garnish as desired and serve.*

VEGAN BROWN RICE &
VEGGIES

	1.5 CUP (3 CUPS COOKED) 1-2 SERVINGS	3 CUP (6 CUPS COOKED) 3-4 SERVINGS	5 CUP (10 CUPS COOKED) 5-6 SERVINGS
BROWN BASMATI RICE, UNCOOKED	1/2 CUP	1 CUP	1 1/2 CUPS
OLIVE OIL	2 tsp	1 TBSP+1 tsp	2 TBSP
KOSHER SALT AND FRESHLY GROUND PEPPER	TO TASTE	TO TASTE	TO TASTE
VEGETABLE STOCK	1/2 CUP	1 CUP	1 1/2 CUPS
WHITE WINE OR WATER	2 TBSP	1/4 CUP	1/3 CUP
LIGHT MISO PASTE (OPTIONAL)	1 TBSP	2 TBSP	3 TBSP
GARLIC CLOVES, CHOPPED	2	4	6
MUSHROOMS, SLICED	1/4 CUP	1/2 CUP	3/4 CUP
FRESH SPINACH LEAVES	1/2 CUP	1 CUP	1 1/2 CUPS
SMALL YELLOW SQUASH, SLICED	1	2	3

Method:

1. Combine all ingredients, except spinach and squash, in the rice cooker and stir.
2. Close lid and press COOK.
3. Cook for 40-45 minutes or until rice cooker switches to WARM.
4. Add remaining ingredients, stir then close lid and press COOK again.
5. Cook for an additional 5-7 minutes or until spinach is wilted and squash is crisp tender.
6. When cooking is complete, garnish as desired and serve.

EASY QUESO
DIP

	1.5 CUP (3 CUPS COOKED) 1-2 SERVINGS	3 CUP (6 CUPS COOKED) 3-4 SERVINGS	5 CUP (10 CUPS COOKED) 5-6 SERVINGS
GARLIC POWDER	1/2 tsp	1 tsp	1 1/2 tsp
KOSHER SALT	TO TASTE	TO TASTE	TO TASTE
HOT PEPPER SAUCE, BOTTLED (OPTIONAL)	TO TASTE	TO TASTE	TO TASTE
HEAVY CREAM	1/2 CUP	1 CUP	1 1/2 CUPS
AMERICAN CHEESE SLICES	12	24	36
MONTERREY JACK CHEESE, SHREDDED	1/2 CUP	1 CUP	1 1/2 CUPS
CREAM CHEESE	2 OZ	4 OZ	6 OZ
TORTILLA CHIPS FOR SERVING	AS DESIRED	AS DESIRED	AS DESIRED

Method:

1. *Combine all ingredients, except the cheeses and tortilla chips, in the rice cooker.*
2. *Stir well, do not cover and press COOK.*
3. *After 6-8 minutes or when mixture simmers, switch rice cooker to WARM and stir well.*
4. *Serve with tortilla chips.*

TIP

Kick this up by adding 1/4 cup canned green chili sauce and 1/2 cup cooked sausage crumbles (you can buy these in 9.6 ounce bags at the grocery store which is a huge time saver).

VEGETARIAN
REISFLEISCH

	1.5 CUP (3 CUPS COOKED) 1-2 SERVINGS	3 CUP (6 CUPS COOKED) 3-4 SERVINGS	5 CUP (10 CUPS COOKED) 5-6 SERVINGS
BASMATI WHITE RICE, UNCOOKED	1/2 CUP	1 CUP	1 1/2 CUPS
VEGETABLE STOCK	1/2 CUP	1 CUP	1 1/2 CUPS
UNSALTED BUTTER OR OIL	1 TBSP	2 TBSP	3 TBSP
KOSHER SALT AND FRESHLY GROUND PEPPER	TO TASTE	TO TASTE	TO TASTE
CHILI FLAKES (OPTIONAL)	TO TASTE	TO TASTE	TO TASTE
PAPRIKA	1 tsp	2 tsp	1 TBSP
WHOLE GARLIC CLOVES, CHOPPED	2 tsp	1 TBSP+1 tsp	3 TBSP
CELERY, CHOPPED	2 TBSP	1/4 CUP	1/3 CUP
YELLOW ONIONS, CHOPPED	2 TBSP	1/4 CUP	1/3 CUP
BELL PEPPERS, CHOPPED	2 TBSP	1/4 CUP	1/3 CUP
MUSHROOMS, CHOPPED	2 TBSP	1/4 CUP	1/3 CUP

Method:

1. Combine all ingredients in the rice cooker and stir well.
2. Close lid and press COOK.
3. Cook for 25 minutes or until rice cooker switches to WARM.
4. Garnish as desired and serve.

TIP

To make this with brown rice or other types of rice, see the reference chart on the tips page 7.

WILD RICE
MEDLEY

	1.5 CUP (3 CUPS COOKED) 1-2 SERVINGS	3 CUP (6 CUPS COOKED) 3-4 SERVINGS	5 CUP (10 CUPS COOKED) 5-6 SERVINGS
WILD RICE, UNCOOKED	1/2 CUP	1 CUP	1 1/2 CUPS
GARLIC CLOVES, CHOPPED	1 TBSP	2 TBSP	3 TBSP
UNSALTED BUTTER	1 TBSP	2 TBSP	3 TBSP
CAPERS, JARRED	1 TBSP	2 TBSP	3 TBSP
KOSHER SALT AND FRESHLY GROUND PEPPER	TO TASTE	TO TASTE	TO TASTE
WATER	1 1/2 CUPS	3 CUPS	4 1/2 CUPS
SMALL CARROT, SLICED	1 CUP	2 CUP	3 CUP
SNOW PEAS, SLICED	1/3 CUP	2/3 CUPS	1 CUP

Method:

1. Combine all ingredients, except carrots and snow peas, in the rice cooker.
2. Stir well then close lid and press COOK.
3. Cook for 55 minutes or until the rice cooker switches to WARM.
4. Gently fold in the carrots and snow peas.
5. Let rest on WARM inside the rice cooker for 5-7 minutes or until vegetables are crisp tender.
6. Garnish as desired and serve.

CHICKEN NOODLE
DINNER

	1.5 CUP (3 CUPS COOKED) 1-2 SERVINGS	3 CUP (6 CUPS COOKED) 3-4 SERVINGS	5 CUP (10 CUPS COOKED) 5-6 SERVINGS
THIN EGG NOODLES, UNCOOKED	1/2 CUP	1 CUP	1 1/2 CUPS
OLIVE OIL	1 TBSP	2 TBSP	3 TBSP
GARLIC CLOVES, CHOPPED	2	4	6
CHICKEN STOCK	1/2 CUP	1 CUP	1 1/2 CUPS
CHICKEN TENDERS, RAW	3	6	9
KOSHER SALT AND FRESHLY GROUND PEPPER	TO TASTE	TO TASTE	TO TASTE
CHILI FLAKES (OPTIONAL)	PINCH	2 PINCHES	3 PINCHES
FROZEN FRENCH CUT GREEN BEANS	1/4 CUP	1/2 CUP	3/4 CUP

Method:

1. Combine all ingredients in the rice cooker and stir.
2. Close lid and press COOK.
3. Cook for 20-25 minutes or until chicken is cooked through and pasta is tender.
4. Spoon onto dishes, garnish as desired and serve.

POLISH KIELBASA
CASSEROLE

	1.5 CUP (3 CUPS COOKED) 1-2 SERVINGS	3 CUP (6 CUPS COOKED) 3-4 SERVINGS	5 CUP (10 CUPS COOKED) 5-6 SERVINGS
RUSSET POTATO, CUBED	1/2 CUP	1 CUP	1 1/2 CUPS
KIELBASA SAUSAGE, CUBED	1 CUP	2 CUPS	3 CUPS
KOSHER SALT AND FRESHLY GROUND PEPPER	TO TASTE	TO TASTE	TO TASTE
YELLOW ONION, SLICED	2 TBSP	1/4 CUP	1/3 CUP
SAUERKRAUT, DRAINED	1/2 CUP	1 CUP	1 1/2 CUPS
ALL PURPOSE FLOUR	1 TBSP	2 TBSP	3 TBSP
HALF & HALF	1/2 CUP	1 CUP	1 1/2 CUPS
CARAWAY SEEDS	1/8 tsp	1/4 tsp	3/4 tsp
BUTTER TYPE CRACKERS, CRUSHED FOR SERVING	AS DESIRED	AS DESIRED	AS DESIRED

Method:

1. *Combine all ingredients, except crackers, in the rice cooker and stir well.*
2. *Cover and press COOK.*
3. *Cook for 20-25 minutes or until potatoes are tender and sauce is thick and bubbly.*
4. *Stir gently, garnish as desired and serve topped with cracker crumbs.*

ONE DISH CHICKEN
FRIED RICE

	1.5 CUP (3 CUPS COOKED) 1-2 SERVINGS	3 CUP (6 CUPS COOKED) 3-4 SERVINGS	5 CUP (10 CUPS COOKED) 5-6 SERVINGS
DARK SESAME OIL	1 TBSP	2 TBSP	3 TBSP
LARGE EGG, BEATEN	1	2	3
KOSHER SALT	TO TASTE	TO TASTE	TO TASTE
CHICKEN TENDERS, RAW, DICED	2	4	6
GREEN ONIONS, SLICED	2	4	6
GARLIC CLOVES, CHOPPED	2	4	6
GINGER COINS, CHOPPED	2	4	6
FROZEN PEAS & CARROT MIX	1/4 CUP	1/2 CUP	3/4 CUP
SOY SAUCE	TO TASTE	TO TASTE	TO TASTE
PERFECT WHITE RICE, COOKED (SEE PAGE 11)	1 1/4 CUPS	2 1/2 CUPS	3 3/4 CUPS

Method:

1. *Pour half of the sesame oil into the rice cooker and press COOK.*

2. *Add the egg and some salt then stir for about 3-4 minutes or until softly scrambled.*

3. *Remove the egg and set aside.*

4. *Add remaining sesame oil, chicken and some additional salt.*

5. *Close lid and cook for 5-7 minutes or until chicken is just cooked through.*

6. *Add remaining ingredients along with the scrambled egg to the rice cooker; stir gently to combine then close lid and press COOK.*

7. *Cook for 5 minutes until mixture is heated through.*

8. *Garnish as desired and serve.*

BONELESS PORK CHOPS
WITH APPLES

	1.5 CUP (3 CUPS COOKED) 1-2 SERVINGS	3 CUP (6 CUPS COOKED) 3-4 SERVINGS	5 CUP (10 CUPS COOKED) 5-6 SERVINGS
BONELESS PORK CHOPS, RAW, THIN CUT	2	4	6
GRAINY MUSTARD, STORE-BOUGHT	1 TBSP	2 TBSP	3 TBSP
SMALL APPLES, SLICED	2	4	6
YELLOW ONION, SLICED	1/4 CUP	1/2 CUP	3/4 CUP
BEER	1/2 CUP	1 CUP	1 1/2 CUPS
LIGHT BROWN SUGAR, PACKED	2 TBSP	4 TBSP	6 TBSP
KOSHER SALT AND FRESHLY GROUND PEPPER	TO TASTE	TO TASTE	TO TASTE

Method:

1. *Place pork in the rice cooker.*
2. *In a bowl, combine remaining ingredients then pour over pork in the rice cooker.*
3. *Close lid and press COOK.*
4. *Cook for 50-55 minutes or until pork chops are tender and sauce is thick and bubbly.*
5. *When cooking is complete, garnish as desired and serve.*

BBQ BEEF
SANDWICHES

	1.5 CUP (3 CUPS COOKED) 1-2 SERVINGS	3 CUP (6 CUPS COOKED) 3-4 SERVINGS	5 CUP (10 CUPS COOKED) 5-6 SERVINGS
BEEF STEW PIECES (CHUCK), RAW, THINLY SLICED	8 OZ	1 POUND	1 1/2 POUNDS
BEEF STOCK	1/2 CUP	1 CUP	1 1/2 CUPS
KOSHER SALT AND FRESHLY GROUND PEPPER	TO TASTE	TO TASTE	TO TASTE
SMOKY BBQ SAUCE, BOTTLED	1/3 CUP	2/3 CUP	1 CUP
BUNS, COLESLAW AND PICKLES FOR SERVING	AS DESIRED	AS DESIRED	AS DESIRED

Method:

1. *Combine all ingredients, except buns, coleslaw and pickles, in the rice cooker.*
2. *Close lid and press COOK.*
3. *Cook for 45 minutes or until beef is tender and liquid is thick and bubbly.*
4. *When cooking is complete, serve on buns with coleslaw and pickles then garnish as desired and serve.*

BOW TIE PASTA WITH CHICKEN &
SUN-DRIED TOMATOES

	1.5 CUP (3 CUPS COOKED) 1-2 SERVINGS	3 CUP (6 CUPS COOKED) 3-4 SERVINGS	5 CUP (10 CUPS COOKED) 5-6 SERVINGS
BOW TIE PASTA, UNCOOKED	3/4 CUP	1 1/2 CUPS	2 1/4 CUPS
CHICKEN TENDERS, RAW	4	8	12
CHICKEN STOCK	1/2 CUP	1 CUP	1 1/2 CUPS
SUN DRIED TOMATO STRIPS, JARRED	1/4 CUP	1/2 CUP	3/4 CUP
WHOLE GARLIC CLOVES, CHOPPED	1	2	3
BROCCOLI FLORETS, FRESH OR FROZEN	1/2 CUP	1 CUP	1 1/2 CUPS
KOSHER SALT AND FRESHLY GROUND PEPPER	TO TASTE	TO TASTE	TO TASTE
GOAT CHEESE	1/4 CUP	1/2 CUP	3/4 CUP
PARMESAN CHEESE, SHREDDED	2 TBSP	4 TBSP	6 TBSP

Method:

1. Combine all ingredients, except the cheeses, in the rice cooker and stir.
2. Close lid and press COOK.
3. When rice cooker switches to WARM (about 25-30 minutes) stir in cheeses until melted.
4. Garnish as desired and serve.

SOURCE PAGE

Here are some of my favorite places to find ingredients that are not readily available at grocery stores as well as kitchen tools and supplies that help you become a better cook.

The Bakers Catalogue at King Arthur Flour

135 Route 5 South
P.O. Box 1010
Norwich, VT 05055

Pure fruit oils, citric acid, silicone spatulas, digital timers, oven thermometers, real truffle oil, off-set spatulas, measuring cups and spoons, knives, ice cream scoops, cheesecloth, cookie sheets, baking pans
www.kingarthurflour.com

Gluten Free Mall

4927 Sonoma HWY Suite C1
Santa Rosa, CA 95409
707-509-4528

All ingredients needed for gluten-free baking
www.glutenfreemall.com

Vanilla From Tahiti

Nui Enterprises
501 Chapala St. Suite A
Santa Barbara, CA 93101
805-965-5153
www.vanillafromtahiti.com

Penzeys Spices

P.O. Box 924
Brookfield, WI 53045
800-741-7787

Spices, extracts, seasonings, seasonal cookie cutters, mallets and more
www.penzeys.com

Chocosphere

P.O. Box 2237
Tualatin, OR 97062
877-992-4623

Excellent quality cocoa (Callebaut)
All Chocolates
Jimmies and sprinkles
www.chocosphere.com

D & G Occasions

625 Herndon Ave.
Orlando, FL 32803
407-894-4458

My favorite butter vanilla extract by Magic Line, cake and candy making supplies, citric acid, pure fruit oils, professional food colorings, ultra thin flexible spatulas, large selection of sprinkles and jimmies, unusual birthday candles, pure vanilla extract, pastry bags and tips, parchment, off-set spatulas, oven and candy thermometers, kitchen timers, meat mallets, large selection of cookie cutters
www.dandgoccasions.com